MW01420020

IT'S NOT YOUR FAULT

A Practical Guide to Navigating the Pain and Problems from Your Parents' Divorce

RESTORED

It's Not Your Fault
Joey Pontarelli

Published by Restored Press
3800 Buchtel Blvd #102202
Denver, CO 80250
RestoredMinistry.com

Edited by Miranda Henkel
Cover by Aleksandar Milosavljevic
Typesetting by Russell Graphic Design

Printed in the United States of America
9798477734191 Paperback

Nihil Obstat: David Uebbing, M.A.
Censor Librorum

Imprimatur: +Most Reverend Samuel J. Aquila, S.T.L.
Archbishop of Denver
Denver, Colorado, USA
May 5, 2023

For my siblings: Anthony, Gerard, Nicholas, Maria, and John Paul.

Watching you suffer has been the hardest part, but I couldn't be more proud of who you've become. You inspire me to be like you and help people like us.

CONTENTS

WHAT HEALTHY COPING LOOKS LIKE

BUILDING HEALTHY RELATIONSHIPS

HEALING TACTICS TO HELP YOU FEEL WHOLE AGAIN

NAVIGATING YOUR RELATIONSHIP WITH YOUR PARENTS

YOUR RELATIONSHIP WITH GOD

DECISIONS AND YOUR FUTURE

INTRODUCTION: HOW THIS BOOK CAN HELP YOU

What's brought the most pain and problems into your life? If you're like me, the answer is the breakdown of your parents' marriage and the loss of your family. Specifically, your parents' separation and divorce. Maybe your parents are still together, but their marriage has brought difficulty into your life. Perhaps you've felt hurt and struggled in various ways, but you've never reflected on how the struggles you face today are intimately connected to the breakdown of your family.

If you can relate, I wrote this book for you. In the pages that follow, you'll receive practical advice on successfully handling the common and unique challenges people like us face.

By reading this book and implementing the advice in your life, you'll see many benefits:

- You'll learn how to cope with your pain in healthy ways instead of unhealthy ones.
- You'll become a better, stronger, and more virtuous person.
- You'll learn to overcome emotional problems.

- You'll be given tactics to build healthy relationships.
- You'll find evidence-based strategies you can use to heal.
- You'll learn how to navigate your relationship with your parents.
- You'll improve your relationship with God.
- You'll make better decisions that build a better future for yourself.
- Most importantly, you'll be given tools and resources to get the help you need.

I Wish I Had This Guide

A guide like this would have been useful for me when I was growing up. When I was eleven, my parents separated. It was extremely painful. My life quickly and dramatically changed for the worse. I felt abandoned, unwanted, and not good enough. I became angry, anxious, depressed, lonely, and hopeless. In an attempt to numb the pain, I turned to pornography and other unhealthy ways of coping. Those coping mechanisms only inflicted more pain and problems. They led me to feeling even more lonely and more lost.

I needed help, so eventually I looked around for resources specifically for people like me. What

I found was shocking and discouraging: Almost nothing practical existed. This baffled me because I personally knew so many people struggling with the negative effects of their parents' separation or divorce. The world, it seemed, had abandoned us and the very real problems we face.

Through trial and error, I learned better ways to handle the pain and problems. But it didn't come easily. I hurt people I loved and made decisions I regret. When I thought the effects of my parents' breakup were behind me, new problems would arise. By far, the area most impacted has been my dating relationships and marriage.

Why I Can Help You

Who am I to write such a book? I am not a psychologist. I do not have my PhD. I'm not a marriage or relationship expert. Here's what I can offer: Almost twenty years of dealing with these challenges personally. I've had more than five years of counseling and ten years of spiritual direction. For the past five years, I've researched this topic, listened to people like us to develop a thorough understanding of the problems we face, and offered personal guidance to teenagers and young adults.

The advice below isn't flawless, but it is useful. Instead of attempting to offer a perfect solution, I share what I've learned along the way so you can avoid the same pain and mistakes. I haven't reached the summit, but I am on the path. Aside from my story, the advice in this book is derived from three other types of sources: research, expert advice, and the numerous stories of people like us. Most importantly, it is based on common sense.

Who It's For

This book was written for Catholic teenagers and young adults. While help is needed for young children and older adults, I feel called and best equipped to serve this audience. However, if you fall outside that demographic, you can absolutely still benefit from the content. Though we focus on that younger age group, older adults have enthusiastically said our content is helpful for them too. In regards to religion, we do plan to release various versions, such as a secular one.

If you aren't from a broken home, you likely love or lead someone who is. You might be that person's parent, cousin, aunt, uncle, friend, or significant other. As a leader, you might be their teacher, coach, pastor, or youth minister. What you hold in your hands is a resource that you can hand them or read yourself to develop a deeper understanding of that person and how to help. That person is very blessed to have you in his or her life. Thank you for being here.

To any parents reading, please know that I am **not** here to shame or demonize you. I am not here to judge you or your specific situation. The only goal is to help your child to cope, heal, and grow. In doing so, I write some uncomfortable truths. Rest assured that ultimately, the Restored team and I want your child to feel whole again and develop a healthier relationship with you.

There are two ways to read this book. First, cover-to-cover like most books. Second, by going to the most relevant questions you're facing right now. It's written so each question and answer stands on its own. I suggest starting with the second method. Whatever you choose, keep this book handy so you can reference it when problems come your way.

Flip-Out Rule

At any point, if you become overwhelmed in reading this book, put it down. Social psychologist James Pennebaker calls it the Flip-Out Rule, which goes like this: If you feel that a particular topic is too much for you to handle, then stop reading and thinking about it for now. If you feel you aren't ready to address a particularly painful topic, then switch gears and focus on something else. When you are ready, then you can come back to this. If you feel that you will flip out, stop reading.[1] Although the topics in this book are heavy and perhaps anxiety-provoking, rest assured that this book is filled with hope and tools you can use right away.

Don't Just Read, Act

The answers in this book aren't complex. They're simple, but not easy to live out. Instead of merely accumulating knowledge, begin to implement this advice into your life. Knowledge is almost always useless without action. It's good if you know it, it's better if you do it.

To make the book even more helpful to you, we've included complimentary bonus material. This includes a recorded talk on how to build a thriving and divorce-proof marriage, a guide to having a difficult conversation with your parents, an extensive list of healthy coping ideas, and much more. Additionally, all the recommended resources mentioned throughout the book are accessible in one easy location alongside the bonus material. To access the bonuses and recommended resources, see page 225.

You Deserve Better

If you're from a broken home, you've likely struggled for too long without anyone to validate your pain and help you. You deserve better. You deserve to feel whole again. You deserve a better future. You are not doomed to repeat the dysfunction you experienced in your family. You are not destined to repeat the mistakes you saw in your parents' marriage. You can write your own story. How? Keep reading. I'm so happy you're here. Let's dive in.

By the way, feel free to reach out to me at any point. I'd love to hear your feedback or questions. You can reach me at Joey@RestoredMinistry.com.

Handling the Trauma of Your Parents' Divorce or Separation

QUESTION 1

What are some of the effects of my parents' divorce?

Enduring your parents' divorce or separation is painful and traumatic. Not only is the breakup and everything that led up to it difficult, it also brings additional pain and problems into your life that last a long time. It's normal to feel alone, depressed, anxious, and lost. Sadly, most of us don't know how to handle the pain and problems. In an attempt to numb the pain, we often turn to coping mechanisms that only work for a short time and that ultimately aren't good for us.

That is Mary's story.* As a little girl, she watched her parents fight almost constantly. Their marriage was a mess. They needed help, but they never got it. Before Mary graduated high school, her mom told her, "I want to divorce your dad." Unsure of what to say, Mary replied, "I just want the fighting to stop." Her mom filed for divorce soon after.

* Names changed to protect privacy here and elsewhere.

What seemed like a solution to a bad situation just made things worse, especially for Mary. Up to that point, Mary didn't act out. She silently held her pain inside. But that all changed when she left for college. She started drinking heavily and dating the wrong guys. She later married one of them. He turned out to be a drug addict and an alcoholic. Their marriage was chaotic, just like her parents' marriage all those years ago.

When she got pregnant, Mary was terrified her baby would grow up in that hell, so she got an abortion. That brought so much more pain into her life. Soon after, she divorced her husband—repeating the cycle started by her parents. And once the dust settled, she fell into a deep depression. Years later, she still deals with emotional problems.

Unfortunately, Mary's story isn't unique. Each year, over one million American children endure their parents' divorce.[2] The research shows that as children of divorce, we are more likely to:[3,4]

- Attempt suicide
- Struggle in romantic relationships
- Get divorced
- Struggle in relationships with our parents

- Experience emotional problems like depression, anxiety, and loneliness
- Struggle with low self-esteem
- Experience health and social problems
- Act out in violence
- Struggle in school
- Not get married
- Not have children
- Drop out of high school
- Not go to college
- Not receive financial support for college from our parents

After studying children of divorce for twenty-five years, Dr. Judith Wallerstein published her findings in the book, *The Unexpected Legacy of Divorce*. In it, she says: "Our findings challenge the myth that divorce is a transient crisis and that as soon as parents reestablish their lives, the children will recover fully. That doesn't happen."[5] She found that the pain and problems from the divorce don't end with the legal proceedings. They endure for years. In fact, Dr. Wallerstein discovered that the full effects weren't experienced until adulthood—called the Sleeper Effect.

Author Leila Miller found that to be true too. She took the stories of seventy adult children of divorce and organized them into a book called *Primal Loss: The Now-Adult Children of Divorce Speak*. Interestingly, most of the contributors were in their 30's, 40's, or 50's. The book details the pain and problems the contributors dealt with for years, often long-removed from the divorce itself.

These sources show us that divorce does real damage to people like us. It doesn't mean we're weak, or that we can't heal from the trauma. It doesn't mean we don't love our parents, and aren't grateful for all they have done for us. But it does mean that we are deeply affected by divorce. As a result, a lot of time and effort needs to go into the healing process.

QUESTION 2

Everyone acts like my parents' divorce isn't a big deal. Is it wrong for me to feel hurt by it?

No, there's nothing wrong with you for feeling hurt by it. In fact, that's the appropriate response. Psychiatrist Viktor Frankl wrote, "An abnormal reaction to an abnormal situation is normal behavior."[6] In other words, feeling hurt by the breakdown of your family is not strange at all. Honestly, it's strange for people to pretend it isn't a big deal. Sadly, the trauma of divorce is minimized in two ways: 1) Sugarcoating, and 2) Gaslighting.

Well-intentioned people sugarcoat when they say, "Look on the bright side. At least it wasn't worse!" or "Now you have two homes and twice as many Christmas presents!" Gaslighting involves manipulating your feelings: They might say things like, "You should be happy about your parents' divorce" or "It's for the best. Everyone is happier." As a result, we conclude we are wrong for feeling hurt, and silently hide our pain.

Another example of sugarcoating that sometimes takes place in religious circles is called spiritual bypassing. It consists of downplaying the impact or sadness of a situation by using spiritual language to make the person being confided in more comfortable. These statements aren't bad and may even be true, such as "God has a plan" or "This is making you holy." But the harm lies in the reason behind saying them, which is not to console or offer real empathy and compassion, but rather to skip over tough issues using sound bites for the comfort of the confidant. Sometimes, well-meaning individuals will make these statements trying to help, but often end up making you feel even worse.

The truth is that divorce feels like the death of your family. As such, it should not be taken lightly. To lessen the blow of divorce, some claim that your family isn't broken. It has merely changed. If that's true, then why is it so painful? Because divorce is an injustice to you. This is why anger is a common and appropriate emotional response, since anger exists to teach us that an injustice has occurred. You deserve two parents—a mom and a dad—who love each other and stick together. That was robbed of you.

One author argued that divorce is actually worse on children than parental death. This may seem like an exaggeration; how can it be worse than the death of a parent? But she explains:

> "Divorce is far harder on children than parental death. Death is recognized as a tragedy, and usually draws survivors closer. [. . .] The surviving parent and the child are united in their bereavement and think back on the late parent with affection. The memory of the deceased parent can even spur the child to try to live in such a manner as would make the late parent proud.
>
> After divorce, the custodial parent and child have markedly different feelings about the missing parent, and as Whitehead notes, the non-residential parent 'who remains remote or absent can be a source of continued torment [to the child] in a way that the parent who dies is not.' And children may feel guilty about longing for a father who is such a source of pain to their mother."[7]

If you feel this way, you are not alone. As a culture, we've become so numb to divorce because it's so common. As a result, there's a huge misunderstanding about how harmful it is to people like us. There's also a belief that children are resilient. It's true that we are resilient, but not as resilient as some like to think. We are breakable. We feel pain. We might bounce back, but it doesn't mean we aren't affected.

QUESTION 3

Is divorce ever the right decision?

When talking about divorce, it's important to distinguish between the civil contract and the actual marriage bond. Before Christian weddings, the couple must obtain a civil marriage license from their local court. After the exchange of vows, that license is signed by the priest or officiant, the couple, and the witnesses—typically the best man and maid of honor. The marriage license is a piece of paper that says you are civilly married. Inversely, a civil divorce is a legal declaration that you are no longer married civilly. The legal marriage contract is severed. However, the actual marriage bond is an entirely separate matter.

The marriage bond is a much deeper spiritual and natural bond between a husband and wife which supersedes any civil law. The marriage bond cannot be broken. It is lifelong and only ends at death (as mentioned in the original wedding vows). A civil divorce merely changes a couple's legal status from "married" to "divorced" but does nothing to end the marriage or excuse them from the vows they made. In other words, a civil divorce changes what a marriage is in the same way that taking off someone's name tag changes who they are. It changes the appearance of the marriage, but not the internal reality of the marriage.

It's clear from Scripture that God "hates divorce."[8] When challenged by the religious leaders of his time, Jesus spoke strongly about the evil of divorce and even declared that whoever divorces his spouse and marries another commits adultery (see Matthew 19:6). The *Catechism of the Catholic Church* teaches that divorce is a "grave offense against natural law," and uses strong language to condemn divorce.[9] At the same time, the *Catechism* says, "If civil divorce remains the only possible way of ensuring certain legal rights, the care of the children, or the protection of inheritance, it can be tolerated and does not constitute a moral offense."[10] Why does the Church condemn divorce, yet still tolerate it in certain cases?

Author Leila Miller says, "The answer lies in our language limitation. We are using (and confusing) the same word, 'divorce,' for two different concepts, two different intents, and two different courses of action."[11] In this sense, she points out that civil divorce is merely a "protective legal maneuver," a separation, available in cases where it is the only possible way to offer protection to a spouse and children, such as in cases of abuse or abandonment.[12] While the legal maneuver is necessary as a last resort, it does nothing to end the marriage bond itself and therefore is tolerated.

On the other hand, divorce pursued as a way to end the marriage bond is never morally allowed. In fact, Miller states that "divorce only *claims* to break marriage but cannot achieve it."[13] Is she exaggerating the Catholic Church's teaching? Surprisingly, no. The Catechism itself points out that divorce merely *claims* to break the marriage contract but cannot actually do so: "It claims to break the contract, to which the spouses freely consented, to live with each other till death."[14] Miller continues, "Catholics may never use civil divorce with the intent to end their marriage (which, as we've seen, is neither moral nor possible)."[15] St. John Paul II points out that, "There is in fact a difference between those who have sincerely tried to save their first marriage and have been unjustly abandoned, and those who through their own grave fault have destroyed a canonically valid marriage."[16]

In short, the Catholic Church maintains that it is not possible to get a civil divorce and thereby end your marriage bond. A legal divorce only *says* you are no longer *legally* married—but the spiritual and natural bond that forms when two people profess marital vows to each other remains. This is why any romantic relationship even after a divorce is considered adulterous. Because the couple is, in fact, still married—even if the court says otherwise.

In that light, you may wonder: what's a struggling couple to do? First and foremost, they should stay true to their wedding vows. If abuse or danger exists, the spouse should *always* get to safety—this should go without saying. In extreme cases, a legal separation might be a necessary measure to protect the spouse from danger or misbehavior and act as a step to heal the marriage. Regardless, each spouse should genuinely exhaust their options to heal the marriage, even if it takes years to do so. A fantastic resource for troubled marriages is *The Alexander House*. Over the past 20 years, Greg and Julie Alexander have coached troubled marriages, helping over 5,000 couples. Their success rate at keeping the couples together and helping to heal the marriage is an astounding ninety-eight percent. You can check them out at TheAlexanderHouse.org or listen to my podcast interview with Greg and Julie at RestoredMinistry.com/30.

By speaking these uncomfortable truths, I am in no way belittling the suffering of spouses in difficult marriages. I've seen how challenging broken marriages can be. It is heartbreaking, but it's wrong to say that broken marriages cannot be redeemed. There are certainly situations that seem hopeless, but stories of toxic marriages redeemed prove that it is possible. For real-life examples of horrible marriages that were saved, you can read the book *Impossible Marriages Redeemed: They Didn't End the Story in the Middle.* A free PDF version is included with the book bonuses at RestoredMinistry.com/bonus.

Even if the marriage is not healed due to the refusal or behavior of one spouse, the abandoned spouse who stays true to his or her wedding vows is truly heroic. St. John Paul II said these spouses "give an authentic witness to fidelity, of which the world today has a great need. For this reason they must be encouraged and helped by the pastors and the faithful of the Church."[17] Staying true to your wedding vows should never be confused with allowing physical or emotional abuse to continue.

Again, in those extreme cases the spouse and children should always get to safety. Careful discernment is needed to determine the appropriate next steps. Thankfully, most divorces are not abusive or violent. According to a leading divorce researcher, it is estimated that 70% or so do not involve abuse or violence.[18] But even in those extreme cases, fidelity to the wedding vows—even from afar—is heroic and necessary.

For situations where a serious barrier prevented a marriage bond from truly existing, Church law—the *Code of Canon Law*—offers a juridical process whereby a Church tribunal determines if a marriage is null (see next question about annulments). For guidance on how to handle those situations where a separation is necessary, read the *Catechism of the Catholic Church* 2382–2386, which can be found online. For more on the topic of when civil divorce is tolerated, search online for Leila Miller's article *When Does the Church Tolerate Divorce?*

QUESTION 4

What is an annulment and how does it work? Will I become an illegitimate child?

It's natural to wonder or worry about being labeled "illegitimate" if your parents get an annulment. Before answering, it's crucial to emphasize that the legitimacy of a child is not a question of dignity or worth. It cannot be overstated that the title of "illegitimate" does not lessen the value of a person in any way. That person is not unimportant or unwanted in the eyes of God or the Church, and shouldn't be treated as such. It's simply a term that reflects the validity of the parents' marriage as it relates to that child's conception or birth. It's more about the parents than the child. In practical terms, being deemed illegitimate today carries no concrete consequences.

But how does legitimacy work? From a Church law perspective, "The children conceived or born of a valid or putative marriage are legitimate."[19] Valid marriages are explained below, but a putative marriage is one that appears valid even though it is later revealed to be invalid. Further, in the eyes of the Church, legitimacy isn't based on civil recognition. A marriage may not be civilly recognized but if recognized by the Catholic Church, children born from it are legitimate. For deeper insights, see the *Code of Canon Law*, 1137–1140.

That aside, annulments are frequently misunderstood as "Catholic divorces." Some claim that this confusion stems from corruption in the annulment process (e.g. giving them out too readily, reserving the process for the wealthy or popular). Regardless, annulments are not Catholic divorces. A divorce is the legal end of a civil marriage contract, but an annulment states the marriage was never valid from its inception. The Church is not saying the lifelong marriage bond can be destroyed, but rather there was no valid marriage bond from the start. In other words, an annulment is a declaration by the Church that a marriage was not validly formed at the time of the wedding vows for various reasons, some of which are covered below.

To better understand annulments, it's helpful to understand what makes a marriage valid. There are four elements of a valid marriage (see the *Catechism of the Catholic Church*, 1625-1632):

1. The spouses are free to marry (i.e. they are not already married).
2. They freely exchange their consent (i.e., there is no coercion).
3. They intend and promise to marry for life, be faithful to each other, and be open to children.
4. Their vows are made in the proper form (i.e., in a Catholic church, in front of a priest or delegate and two witnesses).

The annulment process consists of three primary steps. First, the spouse requesting a declaration of nullity—the petitioner—submits a written testimony about the marriage. Along with the testimony, a list of people familiar with the marriage must be provided. Those people must be willing to answer questions about the spouses and their marriage. The Church court (known as the tribunal) will contact the spouse—the respondent—who has a right to be involved. If the respondent does not want to be involved, the tribunal still allows the case to move forward.[20]

Second, a tribunal official determines which process to follow depending on the information submitted. Regardless of the selected process, both spouses are allowed access to the testimony unless civil law forbids it (e.g. access to therapy records). Each party may also appoint a Church advocate to represent him or her before the tribunal. A third representative, called the defender of the bond, argues for the validity of the marriage bond.[21]

Third, the tribunal decides whether or not the marriage was invalid. If the marriage is declared invalid, the Church is saying that the marriage bond was never properly formed from the beginning. In that case, the petitioner and the respondent are free to marry in the Catholic Church unless an appeal is submitted or the decision includes a prohibition against one or both parties marrying until certain underlying issues have been resolved (see the *Code of Canon Law*, 1682.1).

There are three reasons why a marriage may be invalid: 1) Lack of form, 2) An impediment, and 3) Defect of consent.

Lack of form means that the marriage vows were not made according to Church requirements. The Catholic Church requires Catholics to be married in front of a priest or deacon and two witnesses. If the couple was merely married in front of a justice of the peace or another type of officiant, the marriage is invalid— unless they received a dispensation from their local bishop to marry outside the

Church. However, this does not apply to couples who are not Catholic or even Christian. These couples can marry outside the Church and still have a valid, natural marriage bond (or in the case of two baptized Protestants, even a sacramental one).

An impediment is a serious condition that prevents a marriage bond from forming. There are twelve impediments to a valid marriage bond, which cannot be addressed at length here. Impediments may include a previous marriage bond, sexual impotence, being below the required age of fourteen for women and sixteen for men, or others.

Defect of consent includes serious psychological problems, being drunk during the wedding vows, or any coercion by force or fear. It also covers intentions against contracting a marriage at all, or against the primary purpose of marriage— the good of the spouses and the procreation and education of children— or exclusion of one of the essential properties of marriage (e.g. faithfulness) at the time of making marital vows. Respectively, examples could be a person who is not a U.S. citizen and married to claim a benefit that accrues only to U.S. citizens, an agreement between spouses not to have any children, or the bride and groom agreeing that if things don't work out, they will get a divorce. On the topic of agreeing not to have children, the Church is clear that contraception is grave matter, but it does not result in defect of consent. Finally, the Church always assumes that a marriage is valid unless proven otherwise (see the *Code of Canon Law*, 1060). Likewise, priests, counselors, and lay people should always assume a marriage is valid until proven otherwise. They should avoid making the personal determination that the marriage is probably not valid anyway, which is directly opposed to Church law.

For more nuanced information about the annulment process, impediments, and special cases, read *Annulment: 100 Questions and Answers for Catholics*, by Pete Vere and Jacqui Rapp.

Overcoming Emotional Pain & Problems

QUESTION 5

How can I stop feeling like my parents' divorce was my fault?

You aren't alone in feeling this way. In fact, most people like us feel this way—at least for some time. When my own parents split, I blamed myself too. I felt like I could have prevented it from happening. If only I had said this or done that, perhaps they would not have broken apart.

Why do we blame ourselves? Usually, it is because we feel powerless in a situation we didn't choose or cause. Feeling completely helpless, we grasp for some level of control by convincing ourselves that we could have done something to avoid it all. An even more difficult struggle is accepting the fact that one or both parents, whom we love, would do something that could hurt us so much. It's easier to blame ourselves than to blame them. It's our way of protecting them. Developmentally as children, we lack the cognitive capacity to move out of black-and-white thinking. Forced to choose between ourselves and our caregivers, we will almost always accept the blame. This is done in hopes of maintaining a good image of the people we need to trust in order to feel safe in our unpredictable world. Further, even if we've never consciously blamed ourselves, we may have done it unconsciously which may present itself in feeling that we are somehow bad.

Whether you or maybe someone else wrongly placed the blame on you, it's all a debilitating lie. Believing it will only harm you. Please, hear me:

Your parents' divorce is *not* your fault.

There's nothing you did to cause it. There's nothing you could have done to prevent it. In fact, the problems that caused the split were likely present in your parents' marriage long before you were even born. Sadly, there is nothing you can do to fix it, either. The responsibility is not yours, even if you want it to be.

The uncomfortable truth is that our parent(s) choices hurt us, even if that wasn't their intention. In fact, they probably thought they were doing what was best for themselves and for you. In order to heal, we have to first accept this truth. This is not about blame as much as it is about acknowledging the responsibility of those whose job it was to protect us.

Next time you feel responsible for what happened to your parents' marriage and your family, remember: It wasn't your fault. You couldn't have prevented it. There's nothing you can do to fix it. *It is not your fault.*

Instead, accept the fact that your parents, who would die for you, made choices that harmed you. That was wrong. There's no excuse for it. Their actions damaged you and your family. That's no small deal. In order to heal, you need to face that in all its heaviness. Then, give yourself space to grieve the loss (see page 142). By doing that, you'll be able to forgive your parents and hopefully even build a healthier relationship with them.

QUESTION 6

What can I do to cure my loneliness?

According to research, children of divorce are more likely to struggle with loneliness than children from intact families.[22] To stop feeling so lonely, we first need to understand *why* we feel lonely. Typically, at the core of our loneliness is this belief: I don't belong.

My parents' breakup shattered my trust in them, which led me to pull away from my family. But my loneliness went beyond my family. I felt like I didn't belong among my close friends because I came from a broken home and they did not. Unlike them, I engaged in problematic things to cope with the pain in my life, which left me with feelings of guilt and deep regret. It seemed like none of them could understand; I was an outsider.

The way I presented myself also made me lonely. I presented myself how I assumed people wanted me to be, both in my family and to the outside world. I thought if they saw my brokenness and the mistakes I had made, they would disown me. I was desperate to be wanted, loved, and good enough. But the mask I wore made that difficult, since I felt isolated from others.

We can begin to cure our loneliness once we understand it. In time, I learned I didn't have to remain alone under my mask. There were good people in my life who would love me as I was. Showing the real me made them love me more, not less. I started to be vulnerable in my friendships. My friends proved that I can be loved in spite of my brokenness and mistakes. At times it felt risky to be my true self since there was a chance I could have lost some friends. But in reality, it showed me who my true friends were and who were not.

To help cure your loneliness, look for good friends or a mentor with whom you can be vulnerable. Take it upon yourself to grow in those friendships by making time for them. Plan some fun things to do together: Cook dinner for them, play sports or board games, or check out a restaurant or coffee shop. But don't stay on the surface. Go deeper by asking them questions about their lives and sharing about yours. Developing meaningful friendships will help you feel less lonely.

An article in *Psychology Today* explained a study about loneliness.[23] The study looked at four methods of treating loneliness to find which was the most effective:

1. Improve social skills: Learn how to have a conversation, hold eye contact, ask questions, and pick up on social cues.
2. Enhance social support: Find people who will support you when you're struggling or facing a problem in life.
3. Increase opportunities for social interaction: Attend events, play games, or join a league.
4. Change negative thinking patterns: Research shows that "over time, chronic loneliness makes us increasingly sensitive to, and on the lookout for, rejection and hostility. In ambiguous social situations, lonely people immediately think the worst."[24] In other words, people who feel lonely pay more attention to the negative in social situations. For example, if a lonely person is out with a friend who is acting distant, they may assume they have done something wrong. This causes the lonely person to withdraw and isolate themselves further, which makes them lonelier—creating a vicious cycle.

The study found that changing negative thinking was the most effective method of curing loneliness. According to the article, "[Treatment methods] aimed at changing [negative] thinking patterns were, on average, four times more effective than other [methods] in reducing loneliness. (In fact, the other three approaches weren't particularly effective at all.)"[25]

It all starts with your thoughts. What you think matters. How you live your life is largely a result of your thoughts. When you fall into negative thinking, you need to immediately challenge your negative thoughts. Begin by validating your emotions. Judging or shaming them won't serve you. Remind yourself that it's understandable to think that way and feel that way given what you have been through. Once your emotions are understood and validated, they often settle. To help you, engage your logical mind, so that your emotions don't rule you. When facing a discouraging thought, you should ask: Is that thought actually true? Or is there another way to look at it?

Returning to the example of the distant friend, we should challenge ourselves by asking: Is it possible they may have had a difficult day, their significant other broke up with them, their family is going through a rough time, or, quite simply, they're just tired? Consider other ways to look at the situation. And don't be afraid to ask!

Another helpful tactic when feeling lonely is helping someone who is lonelier. Naturally, we have to be careful that we don't bury our loneliness by helping others. You should see it as a way to help someone else, not merely a way to avoid your own loneliness. While we don't ever want to bury our pain, it sometimes helps to look beyond it. Perhaps that's one definition of selflessness—looking beyond our own pain. It seems counterintuitive, but helping someone else can actually bring relief when you are struggling.

Ultimately, only God can satisfy the ache within our hearts for happiness. More than anyone, turn to God when you feel lonely. Tell him, "God, I feel lonely right now," and ask him to comfort you.

QUESTION 7

How can I better deal with my anxiety?

Anxiety is truly a horrible experience: the tightness in your chest, your thoughts racing, the shortness of breath, the lack of peace, the inability to relax, and the resulting physical and mental exhaustion. After my parents separated, anxiety became a common struggle. At one point in high school, I felt almost constant anxiety for three months.

Anxiety has many roots. In my case, the root was a desire for control. I feared repeating the pain and trauma of my past, so I tried to create a world where that wouldn't happen. Trying to exert that level of control is emotionally and mentally exhausting. It requires you to keep your world small and stay very guarded.

Eventually, I learned that I couldn't control everything, I couldn't avoid mistakes, and I couldn't prevent pain. I learned there are things I can control and things I cannot. For the things I can control, I had to do my best. For the things I could not control, I had to surrender. Once that really sunk in, I experienced peace again and the pressure began to melt away. However, it isn't always that simple. To help, a competent therapist trained in dialectical behavioral therapy (DBT) can assist in this practice of acceptance and change.

In other words, surrender was key to combating my anxiety. To help, I brought my worry to God with simple prayers, such as "Jesus, I give you my anxiety." I'd imagine myself holding the situation in my open hands, offering it to Jesus. Sometimes, I felt that he would take it, but not every time.

In those moments, Mother Teresa's words came to mind, "Accept whatever he gives and give whatever he takes with a big smile." If surrender doesn't work, we need acceptance. I continued to offer the source of my anxiety to God, but if he didn't take away my anxiety, I accepted that. That acceptance brought peace. I trusted God knew better than I did. I struggled to understand why I had to go through suffering, but I had seen too many examples in my own life, in Scripture, and in the lives of the saints that proved he wasn't a careless or cruel God. He wanted the best for me.

Another tactic that helped was getting out of my head. Anxiety, and its sibling OCD, leaves us stuck in our minds. It disconnects us from reality. So I used my senses to bring myself back to real life: touching my desk, listening to good music, tasting delicious food, smelling beautiful flowers, or watching a sunset. Those things helped me escape my racing thoughts and grounded me in the present moment.

Now, these tactics alone won't often cure anxiety. Sometimes, there are psychological and physiological factors that require the guidance of a competent mental health professional. In some cases, medication might also be necessary—ideally combined with therapy. A counselor can help you make those decisions. Find a counselor at RestoredMinistry.com/coaching.

QUESTION 8

I'm tired of feeling depressed. How do I feel happy again?

Depression is a complex psychological condition. There are numerous factors and causes of depression. In some cases, depression is simply a chemical imbalance in the brain. In other cases, depression is situational—brought on by an event or series of events.

Classical psychology, mostly based on Sigmund Freud's ideas, believed psychological problems were caused by the repression of emotion. For example, the repression of anger at your father. Instead of dealing with the difficult emotion, people push it down and avoid it. That repression then causes symptoms like depression, anxiety, or other psychological problems. It seems this is certainly true in some scenarios.

But psychologist Conrad Barrs disagreed with Freud. He believed that most people dealing with psychological problems suffer "Emotional Deprivation Disorder," meaning we didn't receive the love and affirmation we needed, especially as children or adolescents. This causes a seemingly bottomless hole in us that is longing for that need to be filled. The conditions we develop, such as depression or loneliness, are often rooted in that lack of love and affirmation. And so, we need to experience that love and affirmation from our friends, mentors, and ideally our parents.

I've felt depressed at different points in my life. When my parents separated, I felt extremely sad right away. Aside from sadness, I felt broken and hopeless. As mentioned, I once went three consecutive months without feeling much relief or joy. I felt dead inside. And though I've never experienced chronic depression, my moods in college were so drastic that I decided to go back to counseling.

To combat depression, first reflect on whether your depression is chronic or situational. It could be both, chronic and situational, if it stems from the unacknowledged trauma of your parents' divorce that happened many years ago. This might be difficult to determine. If you've felt depressed for more than two weeks, talk to a counselor. They'll help you determine whether your depression is chronic or not. Medication might be necessary in some cases, especially for chronic depression.

In the meantime, two helpful tips to lift your mood are to practice gratitude and to laugh more. Firstly, reflect on what you are grateful for. Harvard researchers have found that gratitude helps your brain focus on the positive, which can make you feel happier.[26] Secondly, laughing is so good for many reasons, especially when you're feeling down. Watch funny shows, movies, videos, or read a book that makes you laugh to feel better.

Most importantly, understand that feeling depressed isn't your identity. It simply describes how you're doing at a particular moment, not who you are. Even if you have chronic depression, you can learn to manage it well and experience all the joys you are meant to experience in life. Take ownership of your depression by making a plan to manage it. Don't let it own you. A counselor can help you make that plan. Then, stick to it. A plan without action is useless.

Ask yourself what your depression may be trying to tell you or bring attention to and begin to treat the root cause of your depression. A friend of mine who struggled with chronic depression for years completely eliminated it by healing her wounds, growing her relationship with God, and taking care of herself.[27] Naturally, it's not always that simple. To learn more, get the book *The Catholic Guide to Depression,* or find a good counselor at RestoredMinistry.com/coaching.

QUESTION 9

I struggle with low self-esteem. How can I become more confident?

Confidence is defined as "a feeling of self-assurance arising from one's appreciation of one's own abilities or qualities."[28] Basically, you know and feel like you have what it takes. People like us are more likely to struggle with low self-esteem.[29] A big reason for this is that our relationship with our parents is so intimately tied to our self-esteem. If a parent has told you that you're useless and worthless in one way or another, then it's going to be really difficult to feel useful and valuable. On the other hand, perhaps their physical or emotional absence left your desire for affirmation unmet. Either way, the most fundamental questions in your heart went unanswered: Am I good or beautiful? Am I loved? Do I have what it takes?

The most confident and secure people are the ones who know they are loved. If our parents don't speak to those fundamental questions, we often feel insecure because we question our lovability.

Self-doubt follows, which causes low confidence. Thankfully, it is possible to become more confident. The foundation of confidence is knowing deep inside that you are valuable and loved.

Your value as a human being is immeasurable. It is greater than all the money in the world. You are worth dying for. If you doubt that, understand that God thinks so. He judged that you were worth him becoming human by suffering brutally and dying just so you'd have a chance to be happy with him forever in Heaven. You are invaluable in the eyes of God. I'm not sure there's a way I can convince you of that through these words, but reflect on them and allow yourself to feel that affirmation.

So much confidence comes from simply being comfortable in your own skin, meaning you don't feel the need to pretend. You don't feel the need to be someone else. That's difficult for people like us. If you were like me, you likely felt the need to pretend to be someone else for both of your parents, your friends, or your relatives. People like us typically become incredibly skilled at recognizing what someone wants us to be and assuming that role. Most often, those people are our parents. We're one person with Mom and a different person with Dad. We're like chameleons—we change to blend in with our environments. It's not easy but we have to learn to be comfortable with ourselves. We have to trust our strengths and accept our weaknesses. If we feel uneasy in a particular situation, that's allowed! There's nothing wrong with that.

Confidence is also built by doing intimidating things and succeeding at them. When I gave my first speech, I was terrified. I felt so nervous that I just read my notes. Looking back, it makes me cringe. But over time, I got better at it. It was always intimidating, but as I did it more, I learned to trust my ability to do it well. The *only* way I could improve my ability? By doing it scared. If I allowed my fear to keep me from doing it, I would not feel as confident as I do now. I still get nervous on stage, but now I have successful memories to fall back on. So, don't let your fear hold you back. Do things scared. Over time, you'll get better at whatever you're doing. As you do, you'll learn to trust your ability, which will make you feel more confident. You'll probably always feel some fear, but your past successes and belief in your ability will help you do it in spite of your nerves or self-doubt.

A helpful tip from sports psychologists is to have a few victories ready to recall. No matter how small, recall the times where you doubted yourself yet gave it your best and succeeded. Keep at least three of these memories easily accessible in your mind to give you confidence when you begin to doubt yourself. You did it then, you can do it now too. Along with those memories, say positive things to yourself. Even if you're unsure, tell yourself that you can do it. The words we say to ourselves are powerful.

Another obstacle to becoming confident is comparison. It's easy to see others' positive qualities and your negative qualities. The things they are doing right and you are doing wrong. Everything they have (an intact family, wealth, your dream job . . .) and you do not. It can feel like you'll never measure up. But comparison never works because you only see what others *want you to see.* Most people don't post about their serious character flaws on social media. They don't post their bloopers; they post their highlights. Comparison is also a trap because it's impossible for you to *be someone else.* Admiring others is good and very helpful, but at the end of the day, we have to focus on being the best version of *ourselves*—not a seemingly flawless influencer that we only know through our feed. So, consider what the best version of yourself looks like, and what is standing in the way of becoming that person. Instead of comparing yourself to everyone else, compare yourself to the person you were yesterday. It's a lifelong journey but you do have what it takes to grow a little bit every day! The more you're doing to be the best you can be, the better you will feel about who you are.

Don't feel the need to be perfect. You are going to mess up. That's okay. Get comfortable trying and failing. If you fall, get up, and keep going, then you've won. Give yourself permission to be imperfect. Put in the hard work to become competent in whatever area of life—sports, school, music, relationships, and anything else. Competence is acquired through coaching and repetition. By becoming competent, you'll feel more confident.

QUESTION 10

After my family broke apart, I felt abandoned, unwanted, inadequate, and even rejected. Is something wrong with me?

No. Your family is the fundamental foundation of your life. When it breaks apart, you are left with many wounds, including feeling abandoned, unwanted, not good enough, or rejected. The stories we've heard almost always share those themes. So if you feel that way, you're not alone.

To be clear, your parents have zero intention of hurting you. On the contrary, they would likely die for you. In fact, they probably genuinely believe the divorce is in your best interest. But if every parent truly knew the hidden and painful effects, divorce would be much less popular. Separation would only be used in extreme cases like abuse.

Even so, you have to acknowledge that the actions of one or both parents harmed you. You might feel abandoned because perhaps one parent physically departed from your life while the other left emotionally. You might feel unwanted because you don't get the attention or love you crave from your parents. You might feel rejected or not good enough because they chose another life, person, family, or simply their own desires, over you.

The good news is these wounds are possible to heal.

In episode two of the podcast, *The Place We Find Ourselves*, counselor Adam Young explains the six things every child needs from his or her parents:

1. Attunement
2. Responsiveness
3. Engagement
4. Regulate our Affect
5. Strength to Handle our Negative Emotions
6. Willingness to Repair the Relationship

Attunement is a parent's ability to read what is going on inside of you—what you're thinking and feeling. It involves noticing when something changes in you. He says, "a parent that is distracted by their own needs and personal pains cannot be attuned to their child's pains."[30] In a nutshell, this partially explains why divorce is so harmful. Aside from breaking apart the parents and family, it triggers a host of pain and problems that cause parents to focus on themselves instead of their children.

Responsiveness is your parents' positive response to what they noticed happening in you. Children need their parents to comfort and reassure them when something is wrong. When you were sad or numb, you needed them to help comfort you. When you were anxious or panicked, you needed them to help calm you. Your parents' actions or lack of actions in response to your needs made you feel loved and secure or unloved and insecure.

Engagement is similar to responsiveness, but it is proactive. It involves the desire, intention, and action of your parents to know your heart. Adam Young asks, "Were you pursued by your parents on the level of your heart?"[31] If your parents didn't attune to you, didn't respond when you needed them, and failed to engage you on the level of your heart, you likely felt abandoned.

Your "**affect**" is your internal emotional state. Regulating your affect means your parents had the ability to bring peace and calm when you felt uneasy. Young explains that there are two ends of the spectrum—terrified or panicked, to numb or shut down. When you feel stress, your internal emotional state is "dysregulated." As a child, your ability to manage your affect was very limited. If your affect or mood wasn't regulated by your parents, then you would have been forced to regulate it yourself—an almost impossible task for a young child. You can't learn to do it well by yourself because you learn by watching Mom or Dad do it.

Having the **strength to handle your negative emotions** well is not an easy skill for parents. A mistake many parents make is not allowing their children to feel negative emotions. For example, always telling a child to stop crying or being angry—instead of validating those emotions, giving them the freedom to feel them, and even showing them how to express them in a healthy way. Speaking about the inability of some parents to handle negative emotions, Adam Young powerfully says, "Perhaps your family was too fragile to bear the weight of your unedited soul."[32]

Lastly, you needed your parents to be **willing to repair** or make amends when there was a disconnection or hurt in the relationship. When they failed you, did they try to make it right by apologizing? Young says that it's completely understandable that parents fail. It's expected.

The key is rectifying the relationship. He says, "A healthy relationship is not built on the absence of failure, but on the willingness to own and rectify the failures when they do occur."[33]

Reflect on those six things you needed from your parents. In what ways were these needs met? In what ways were you neglected? How did the breakdown of your parents' marriage play a role in that, regardless of your age? It can be hard to face, but try to be brutally honest. Take some time to reflect through journaling and then try sharing your reflections with someone you trust.

Given these truths, it makes so much sense that you are hurt by your parents' broken marriage. Not only is it more likely that our needs were not met, but such a fundamental need and right to have a mom and a dad have been taken away. When that happens, the consequences are devastating.

QUESTION 11

How do I deal with my anger so it doesn't control me?

Anger has the ability to weaken our self-control and dictate our actions. Its potent effect doesn't need to be explained to anyone who has felt it. But what exactly is anger? Simply put, anger is a heightened emotion you feel in response to a real or perceived injustice. Though it's natural to look down on anger if you saw it managed poorly, it's important to remember that anger has a purpose. Its existence isn't a flaw in you. In fact, feeling angry is a sign that you are functioning properly.

After my parents separated, I became very angry. I acted out. My anger got so bad that I had to attend "anger management" therapy—no joke. Though embarrassing and difficult, I eventually got my anger under control as a teenager.

While you often can't control whether you feel anger, you can control what you do about it. That's not an easy task—especially because when you're angry, as one counselor told me, your IQ drops about 30 points. Most people have an average IQ of 100. A 30-point drop puts you roughly at a 70 IQ, which psychologists say is about the level of mental disability. In other words, you are seriously impaired to make good judgments when you are acting out of anger.

When you feel angry, you need to find a way to calm yourself down so you can choose the right response. Psychiatrist Viktor Frankl offers a simple tip to do that: "Between stimulus and response, there is a space. In that space is our power to choose our response. In our response lies our growth and our freedom."[34] The trick is to master the space between stimulus, whatever it is that makes you feel something, and the response or action you take in reply. To begin mastering it, start by lengthening that space between stimulus and response. Next time you begin to feel angry, take a deep breath. Pause before saying or doing anything. If needed, physically take a step back. This will allow you to calm and regain control of yourself, so you can choose the appropriate response that you won't regret.

Dr. Gary Chapman, author of the *The 5 Love Languages*, offers a five step process for dealing with your anger:[35]

- Consciously acknowledge to yourself that you are angry
- Restrain your immediate response
- Locate the focus of your anger
- Analyze your options
- Take constructive action

Another wise tactic is to write what you feel or talk to a friend about it. It's been said that when we don't express our emotions in words—either in writing or speaking—they usually come out in less helpful ways, such as rage. So remember: your anger isn't bad. It exists for a reason, to point us toward righting an injustice. Allow yourself to feel it, but don't let it control your actions.

QUESTION 12

Self-harm is my way of coping. How do I stop?

A study of 1.3 million people born in Denmark examined whether children of separated parents were more likely to inflict self-harm. Among other things, the researchers looked at who the child was living with at their 15th birthday. They found that, "Those separated from their mother or their father had a more than doubled risk, and children separated from both parents had the largest risk elevation (5–6 times higher) [of inflicting self-harm] compared to those living with both parents."[36]

Why do we hurt ourselves? An obvious explanation is relief. We naturally look for relief when we feel pain. For some people, that relief is pleasure. Feeling good overrides the bad. But for other people, more pain offers relief—sometimes the only relief they feel they can find. The pain overrides other difficult emotions. Another common reason for self-harm is to feel alive. So often, our emotions shut down when we experience trauma.

We feel numb and lifeless. And so, any sensation becomes desirable, even pain. Punishing ourselves is perhaps the most complex reason for self-harm. Often, it is born out of self-hate. It usually implies that we believe we deserve to be punished.

How do you stop? Before diving into that, if you're in a situation where you need immediate help, text HOME to 741741. This crisis hotline offers free, 24/7 support.[37] They won't judge; they just want to help.

Stopping self-harm can feel impossible, but it's not. People quit everyday. It won't be easy, but imagine how your life would be if you found better ways to deal with your pain than harming yourself. Imagine using a healthy technique to find similar relief. Wouldn't you want that instead?

A few immediate tactics experts offer to overcome self-harm:[38]

- Identify the reason and function of your self-harm: What does it do for you?
- Name your reason for quitting
- Identify other ways of achieving the same result
- Tackle the underlying emotions
- Most importantly, and if nothing else, tell someone you trust, because this problem is too

much to overcome by yourself

If self-harm is a habit—it has happened regularly within the past 6 months and your ability to say no is impaired—you need professional help. That can be difficult to admit. But it's not shameful or a sign of weakness to ask for help when you need it. In fact, it's a sign of humility and strength. You can find a counselor at RestoredMinistry.com/coaching.

Right now, get rid of anything you might use to harm yourself. But don't just get rid of the familiar stuff. There is a danger that if you only remove familiar things, you'll use something that you're not familiar with and hurt yourself more. So make it difficult for yourself to access those things. Ask a trusted friend to hold onto those things.

For other options to cope in healthy ways, see page 80.

QUESTION 13

I don't want to live anymore. What hope is there for me?

When life's pain and problems overwhelm you, it's easy to think "I'd be better off dead." Like you, I've been in some dark and empty places. Tempted to despair. Ready to give up. So, I feel your pain. I've lost people I loved to suicide. I've sat with people on the brink of suicide. It's hard to describe the feeling of looking into the eyes of someone you love who is battling to just have the will to live. I am so sorry for what you're going through. It shouldn't be like this. Feeling on the edge of despair without anyone to rescue you is a scary place to be.

Is there hope? Absolutely. The first thing to know: It's usually not that you want to die, but you just don't want to live *with the pain.* You want the pain to end and you think killing yourself is the only way to stop it. That's understandable, but it is a lie. It's *not* the only way to solve your pain. If you could snap your fingers so that the pain and problems went away, wouldn't you want to live? Most difficulties do pass with time.

If you're thinking about killing yourself now, get immediate help. You don't have to endure this alone. There are people who want to help. In fact, that's why the 988 Suicide & Crisis Lifeline exists. Call, text, or chat now:

- English & Español: 988
- Deaf & Hard of Hearing: Use your preferred relay service or dial 711 then 988
- Chat online at 988Lifeline.org/chat

It's confidential and totally free. Trained and caring people are available 24/7. If you call, it works like this:[39]

1. Hear an automated message & options
2. Hold music will play while they connect you
3. A trained counselor will answer
4. They will listen to you to understand your problems, provide support, and share any resources to help you

You don't have to be on the brink of suicide to contact the lifeline. If you feel lonely, depressed, or are struggling with mental illness, substance abuse, or anything else, reach out to them. If you want to know more before you call, you can go to 988Lifeline.org. But do not hesitate to contact them, even if you're unsure if you need it. The relief you will feel after will be worth it. Don't try to solve this on your own. Get help. Call, text, or chat now.

A few additional things you can do:

- Get rid of anything you'd use to kill yourself. Throw it away or give it someone you trust, at least temporarily.
- Talk to a wise, trustworthy person about what you're feeling, no matter how humbling or scary that might be. Message, call, or ask them: Can I talk to you about something serious? If they aren't available, don't stop. Find the next best person.
- During that conversation, thank them for talking to you and ask their permission to open up about something you're struggling with. Bluntly tell them what you're feeling. That act alone will help.
- To prepare for future temptations to suicide, make a list of people in your notes app that you

can call when you're down. A few people to rely on is better than one or two.

- What makes you not want to die? What would it take for you to continue living? Write down those reasons, so you can review them anytime you feel suicidal.
- Find a counselor to talk with that we trust, vet, and recommend at RestoredMinistry.com/coaching
- Get rid of drugs and alcohol. If you're on a prescription drug, don't stop that immediately but call your doctor to assess whether that drug is contributing to your suicidal thoughts. You'd be surprised how many drugs have suicidal thoughts as a side effect. I once spoke to a young man who felt extremely depressed and even struggled with suicide. One day, he learned that a hair product he used had a side effect of depression.
- Download an app, such as *notOK*, to automatically notify close friends or family with the push of a button when you're struggling and help is needed.

For those supporting someone with suicidal thoughts, we often assume that asking directly about those thoughts and validating the feelings beneath them (exhaustion, despair, self-loathing, overwhelm) will lead someone to end their life. This is not founded. In fact, having space to openly and honestly externalize suicidal thoughts and the feelings beneath them can help a person come to greater clarity about their reasons for living. It is often helpful to ask, "what has helped you keep yourself alive and safe so far? Who do you live for?"

You don't always have to feel this way. Killing yourself is not the only way to end the pain and problems. With the right help, you can learn better ways to handle it all. You are *not* alone. People like you, on the brink of suicide, have gotten past it. I know it feels impossible, but it is not. Psychiatrist Viktor Frankl ran a clinic in Vienna, Austria to treat suicidal patients. He used a therapy called Logotherapy. In essence, he helped men and women find a reason to live that was bigger than themselves. It's said that he never lost a single patient. That can be your story, too. Take the first step and ask for help. You are loved and your life is worth living. This isn't it; your story doesn't end here.

What Healthy Coping Looks Like

QUESTION 14

How can I cope in healthy ways instead of unhealthy ways?

After my parents separated, I acted out. I became bitter, angry, anxious, and depressed. In an attempt to numb the pain, I turned to pleasure. A friend introduced me to pornography. Immediately, I felt amazed yet ashamed at what I saw. It quickly led to a habit that offered an escape from the pain and problems in my life.

Though it offered a distraction, I noticed that in the moment it felt so good, but afterward I just felt so empty. Even at a young age, I knew I wanted to be happy. Porn wasn't making me happy, so I needed to change.

The most immediate thing that helped was getting new friends, which is easier said than done. I realized my sports buddies weren't good for me. Luckily, I met new friends who were genuinely happy. Whatever they had, I wanted it. I discovered that the source of their joy was their faith. They were devout Catholics. In an attempt to be like them, I began to learn my faith, develop intimacy with God through prayer and the Sacraments, and even build virtue in my life. The people you surround yourself with are very important. I love the quote, "You can't *change the people* around you, but you can change the people *around you*."

Even with good friends, life is full of stress, intense emotions, and difficult situations. When you experience those difficult things, you react instinctively. That's the definition of coping. Automatically, you usually turn to unhealthy things or use good things excessively. Why? It's simple. When you feel bad, you want to feel good—even if it hurts you in the long run. You want the momentary relief—a distraction, an escape, a way to bury your feelings or the reality of the situation.

The first solution to unhealthy coping is developing "emotional agility." In her book, *Emotional Agility*, Harvard psychologist Dr. Susan David explains that emotional agility has two parts: 1) The ability to face and feel your emotions, and 2) Choosing a response in a way that aligns with your deepest held beliefs.[40] How do you develop emotional agility? Dr. David gives a few tips.

First, she says to create a space between stimulus and response. As quoted before, psychiatrist

Viktor Frankl said, "Between stimulus and response, there is a space. In that space is our power to choose our response. In our response lies our growth and our freedom." In other words, if you want freedom and growth, you need self-mastery. To do so, simply lengthen the space between when you feel something and when you respond. In that space, build discipline to choose what is good and healthy for you instead of what is harmful.

Second, she says to remember that you are not your thoughts. You are not your feelings. You have thoughts. You have feelings. But you are not them and they are not you. They describe how you're doing, not who you are. And they certainly don't control you. With practice, you can learn to control your response to those emotions so they don't own you.

Third, she suggests labeling your emotions. She shares a story about a client named Thomas, who was a business executive. Upon arriving to the office one day, he had a seizure. The paramedics took him to the hospital. After running tests, the doctors had good news: It was extremely unlikely for Thomas to have another seizure. But he wouldn't listen. Thomas became so obsessed with the fear of having another seizure that he lost his job, his wife, and even his home.

Years later, he was living on the streets when Dr. Susan met with him in therapy. She noticed that when asked how things were going, he would almost always reply with "fine." One day, she asked him about his mother. She had been there for him when everyone else abandoned him. When Dr. David asked him how things were going with his mom, Thomas just replied, "Fine. She died." Dr. David was blown away. At that moment, she realized that Thomas suffered from a condition called alexithymia, the inability to identify and put emotions into words. As a result, he continued to struggle and feel stuck in life.

To avoid getting stuck emotionally, Dr. David advises to first learn to recognize your emotions. When you feel angry, acknowledge it to yourself. Then, put your emotions into words by writing or speaking about them with someone else. Describe them in as much detail as possible. That alone is extremely helpful in avoiding unhealthy coping that you'll later regret.

Similarly, allow yourself to feel your feelings. Don't bury them. Don't ignore them. Face them. Instead of running from them, sit with those messy and uncomfortable feelings. If you ignore them, they tend to be prolonged. Like a weed that isn't pulled by its root, they'll keep sprouting up.

When trying to stop unhealthy coping behaviors, remember there are three parts to a habit: 1) The cue or trigger, 2) the routine or behavior, and 3) the reward. Eating fast food is a good example of how the three parts work. When you feel hungry you experience the cue or trigger. Going to get food at a fast food restaurant and eating that food is the routine or behavior. The reward is the pleasure from tasting the food, the feeling of being full, and the nutrients that your body gets.

To change a bad habit, it's almost impossible to stop cold turkey. The neural pathway has already been carved into your brain. As a result, you still experience the trigger (e.g. hunger) and you still desire the reward (e.g. tasty food, feeling full, etc). To change, you have to substitute the routine or behavior with a better action that offers a similar reward. To stop eating unhealthy fast food, for example, you need to substitute that behavior with eating healthy food that offers a similar reward—it tastes good, you feel full, and your body gets the nutrients it needs.

Also, don't get discouraged when you relapse. It happens. Since your brain is so accustomed to that behavior, it's easy to fall back into old ways. Get yourself back up and begin again like you never fell. Discouragement destroys progress more than mistakes do.

For more practical ideas on coping in healthy instead of unhealthy ways, see the bonus material.

QUESTION 15

What's your advice for navigating the holidays and other life events?

During the holidays, coming from a broken family is even more difficult. It's a stark reminder that your parents aren't together and your family is broken. It's common to feel alone and uncertain of how to deal with it all. Logistically, it is challenging to balance time between each parent and twice as many festivities, especially if they don't live in the same area. It's easy to feel pressured to choose sides and pick between parents. While you try to make everyone happy, it becomes overwhelming to balance everyone's desires and expectations. If the divorce was relatively recent, the drama and tension might be especially high, which makes it all the more challenging. Instead of enjoying the holidays, you dread them. But my hope is that the advice below will help you handle the season and even experience some holiday joy again.

First, remember that it's not your responsibility to make everyone happy. It's not your job to fix your parents. It's not your job to clean up the mess inside your family. Although you love your parents, you have to remember that *your parents got themselves in this situation. Now, they need to deal with the consequences.* You can't change them. You can't change your family. Sure, you can positively influence them, but within limits. Don't feel ashamed about spending time with one parent during the holidays. You're not betraying the other parent. You deserve a relationship with both parents. Around this time of year especially, your parents and other people might expect you to put on a good face and be happy. That's not right. You should never have to pretend to be happy in the midst of a difficult situation. Remember that you can't make everyone happy, nor should you try. When you try to make everyone happy, you'll end up making no one happy and yourself miserable.

Second, set and enforce healthy boundaries. Boundaries define what you like and dislike, what you are willing and unwilling to do. They're rules that inform people how to treat you. In a way, they're like the out-of-bounds markers on a sports field. When it comes to the holidays, it's okay to lay down those rules with your parents. Boundaries give people the option to self-select out from a relationship with you if they are not followed.

So, think through what you will allow and not allow. For example, you can tell Dad that you won't talk to him about Mom, or you can set rules about how much time you'll spend with each parent this holiday season. Boundaries are especially important to protect you from manipulative people who want to control you for their own benefit by using fear, guilt, or a sense of obligation. If you're faced with someone like that, back out of the situation or confront them and be clear that you won't allow this to happen. It takes courage, but in the long run, it is worth the discomfort. As part of your preparation, be ready for the predictable circumstances that will arise—a conflict with a specific relative, Dad or Mom bringing their new partner to the party, or whatever else. Prepare for what you'll say and how you'll handle those situations. One option is to avoid the situation altogether. Another is to prepare polite yet firm talking points, so you're not taken by surprise. It doesn't have to be complicated, it just takes some forethought. Lastly, boundaries need to be enforced. If you tell someone, "This is the boundary," and they break it, there need to be consequences. Without them, they'll ignore your boundaries next time. Be ready to enforce any boundaries you set.

Third, communicate ahead of time. Make a plan for the holidays and tell your parents. Avoid spending time with both parents on the same day. On Thanksgiving, perhaps you spend it with your dad. On Christmas, perhaps you spend it with your mom. But the day following each holiday, you can have a second celebration with the other parent. This prevents you from becoming emotionally exhausted, which you have a duty to avoid. Similarly, you have every right to express your feelings to your parents. Be honest and tell them your needs. You can say, "I love you, but it can be really hard around the holidays to please you both and not offend you. I need you to understand my decisions, my boundaries, and understand that the tension in our family makes it difficult to enjoy the holidays."

Set expectations well in advance so nothing comes as a surprise. Tell both parents when you'll see them and for how long. If you live at home, this can be extra difficult. You might not be able to leave a party. But even in that case, communicate what you are and are not comfortable with. Do what's within your power to enforce those boundaries even if they won't respect them. In some cases, you may even need to take a break from visiting certain family members during the holidays, and may benefit from being around other families to remind you that there can be stability that you long for and so deserve.

Fourth, take ownership. While you didn't cause the situation, you can choose how to handle it well. Even amidst the drama and tension, you can choose your response. Do what you can with what you're given. Avoid being the victim who blames and never takes responsibility for what's in their control. One way to take ownership is to plan distractions from the drama, such as watching a movie, spending time with friends, playing games, or another wholesome activity that relieves some of the tension and drama. Avoid isolating yourself for extended periods of time as much as you can. Taking a walk to get a breather is okay, locking yourself in your room for hours at a time is not.

Fifth, be virtuous. In each situation, do your best to respond well. Be diplomatic. Be the better person. Apologize when you make mistakes. Keep in mind that your parents are learning to navigate the holidays too, so give them some grace. Do your best to be kind, loving, and polite. But don't be a doormat. If someone mistreats you, stand up for yourself. Play your role in keeping the peace, but remember you can only play a part. You're not solely responsible for keeping the peace. Most of all, do your best not to allow other people to determine your peace and happiness. Make the decision to keep your calm, whatever the circumstances. In difficult moments, remember to take a breath, pause to think, and detach from the intensity of the emotions before you act. By doing that, you'll make better decisions about what to do and say next.

Sixth, make a plan to take care of yourself. The holidays are emotionally exhausting. If you don't take care of yourself, you might end up doing something you'll regret in an attempt to fill your needs. Think ahead about the difficult emotions you might feel. Have one or two ways to calm yourself if you are anxious, or to experience some joy if you feel down and depressed. (See page 80 about coping in healthy ways instead of unhealthy ways.) Having a plan goes a long way when you feel out of sorts because of the tension, drama, or sadness around the holidays. In the middle of parties or gatherings, don't hesitate to step away for a breather. If you need to leave then do so. Whatever you do, allow yourself to feel your feelings. Work through them. Pay attention to them and learn from them. Ignoring them or stuffing them away only makes things worse. The only way to heal and grow is by moving through those negative and messy emotions. Ask someone to be there for you during the holidays, so you can talk about it all. Don't do this alone.

Seventh, focus on the celebration. Focus on the meaning of the holidays. For example, on Thanksgiving, reflect on what you are grateful for. Even in the worst situations, you can always find something you are grateful for. It's so easy to lose the meaning of the holiday in the midst of the drama and tension. But refocus when needed. Appreciate the little things, especially the food, your siblings, or your pets. Keep in mind that you might need to lower your expectations for the holidays, unfortunately. You might not feel the same joy, safety, and security with your parents anymore. In the midst of that, try to focus on the celebration and the meaning of the holiday.

Eighth, ask God for help. Again, don't do it alone. God sees your pain. He wants to be there for you. Let him. During that family party when you feel alone, tell Jesus about it. Know that he doesn't want it to be this way either. Trust that he's not finished with you or your family. While the divorce or separation is devastating, God can bring good even out of evil. Perhaps you'll never see that in your family, but you can see it in your own life. Trust that he isn't finished with you. Lean on him when things are difficult during the holidays.

Ninth, learn from it all. Whatever happens in life, there are always lessons to learn. See it as an opportunity to become a better, stronger person. Think about the lessons you can use in the future, especially to build your own family. Holiday traditions in your family might die because of the divorce. That's hard to swallow. But remember that you can start your own traditions, especially if you have your own family or soon will. A new tradition might look like spending time with another family or friend if your family is toxic. Be intentional about who you choose to spend time with. Ideally, choose a family that models what it means to be a true and good family—the kind you want for your future. In making your own traditions, think back to what you loved or what you missed out on. Make a list of things you want to do for your own kids one day.

If you simply drift through the holidays without a plan or preparation, then it's likely the drama, tension, and dysfunction will overwhelm you. Given that, it's completely understandable to dread the holidays. But there is a better way. Use the tips above to reduce the drama and enjoy the holidays again. Have hope that you're not doomed to experience holiday distress forever. You can experience the peace and joy you desire during the holiday season.

For more tips on navigating the holidays, listen to this Restored podcast episode: RestoredMinistry.com/32. If you'd like a private place to talk about the challenges that you face during the holidays, join our private and free online community. It's built for people like us. It'll help you feel less lonely, get advice from people who've been through your experiences, and challenge you to grow into a better, stronger person. Join in three easy steps at RestoredMinistry.com/community.

QUESTION 16

I often neglect my needs. How can I do a better job of taking care of myself?

Self-care is a non-negotiable part of life. However, if you are from a broken family, you likely tend to neglect your needs. You don't take care of yourself. Why? Often, you were never taught how to take care of yourself. Perhaps your parents were too occupied with their own lives and so they neglected to meet your needs. Perhaps they neglected their own needs, so the example ingrained in you is to neglect yours too. Another possibility is that, even if you were taught how to care for yourself, you've become so accustomed to caring for others' needs (e.g. parents and siblings) that you forget your own legitimate needs in the process. Tragically, you might even believe that you're not worth taking care of. You might feel like you're not good enough and question your value as a person.

Whatever the reason, if you don't look after yourself it will leave you depleted to the point where you have nothing left to give. Thankfully, you can learn to take care of yourself and love others at the same time.

There are four aspects to the human person: physical, spiritual, emotional, and intellectual. In other words, you need to take care of your body, soul, heart, and mind.

Your body needs four primary things:

- Quality sleep
- Sufficient amounts of water
- Nutritious food
- Daily exercise

If you take the time to focus on even one of these, especially the most neglected item, you'll see the difference and start feeling better about yourself almost right away. Our bodies are precious and deserve to be taken care of, not taken for granted. There are many resources out there to help you understand the details of each of these needs, so pick one and start learning!

Next, you need to take care of your soul. In our modern world, this part of us is neglected the most. As Catholics, we believe that the oxygen of our souls is God's grace. Grace is God's life inside of us. It does many things for us, but primarily it helps us to do good and avoid evil. Grace builds on nature, so if we aren't attending to our physical and emotional needs, our spiritual needs will be much more difficult to meet through spiritual means alone. That being said, here is what will help you take care of your soul:

- Receive the sacraments as often as possible—especially Confession and Communion.
- Make time for personal prayer (just talking to God) every day.
- Read the Bible.
- Read good spiritual books—especially about the saints.
- Learn your faith by asking questions and making time to study it.

You also need to take care of your heart. At the core of this need is the need for love and intimacy. More than anything, you long to be seen, known, and loved. In fact, that need is so potent that people are willing to do all sorts of crazy things in an attempt to just *feel* seen, known, and loved—even if it's not authentic. Instead of settling for the counterfeit, learn to develop true intimacy with people. To take care of your heart:

- Invest in your friendships by spending quality time with friends and opening up to them.
- Invest in mentor relationships. A mentor is typically someone who you want to be like that is older and wiser than you.
- Invest in romantic relationships. These typically are more difficult for people like us who need to put in the time and effort, especially if you're married.
- Invest in your family relationships. Research from Harvard shows that the greatest indicator of happiness is close social connections, especially with your family.[41]

Lastly, you need to take care of your mind. Your mind is like a knife. If you don't sharpen it, it will become dull. Typically school keeps our minds stimulated and hopefully sharp. But when you graduate, it's so important to keep learning. That could be formal learning, such as classes, a certification, or some form of training. It could also be informal learning, such as books, podcasts, movies, documentaries. An often overlooked way to keep your mind sharp is through games, such as chess, strategy board games, or sports that involve more of your mind (e.g. golf, baseball, etc). Hobbies that keep your mind sharp are very valuable, such as playing music, puzzles, or even juggling.

The blunt truth is that if you don't take care of your needs, that part of yourself will continue to deteriorate. Worse, if you wait for someone to fill the needs that you are responsible for filling, you'll be waiting a long time—and you will damage yourself in the process, through neglect. Even though you may struggle to meet your needs since you are still angry that your parents didn't do so for you, now is the time to take your power back by taking care of your own needs and seeing yourself as effective in doing so.

But if you do take care of the legitimate needs of your body, soul, heart, and mind, you'll be happier, healthier, and whole. Further, by taking care of your needs in healthy ways, the temptation to cope with the pain and problems of life in unhealthy ways will be reduced substantially. Make a simple plan to begin taking care of the part of you that is most neglected right now. Do one thing this week to take care of yourself.

Building Healthy Relationships

In this section, the focus is primarily upon romantic relationships and marriage. Why? Because those are the types of relationships most impacted by our parents' divorce or separation. Understandably, not everyone wants to get married. Also, not everyone is called to marriage. It requires discernment, which is discussed on page 204. Even if you don't see marriage as an option for you, many of the principles below apply to other relationships too, such as friendships.

QUESTION 17

How do I avoid repeating my parents' mistakes, and build a healthy marriage?

I remember asking myself this same question as a fourteen-year-old when I started to like this great girl. The idea of repeating what I saw in my parents' marriage terrified me. I wanted authentic love, but I had no idea how to build it. Looking around, I saw plenty of broken or mediocre marriages, but very few great ones that I wanted to mimic. This set me on a quest to learn how to build love that lasts. I found answers in the Church's wisdom, in research, in observing great couples I eventually met, and through trial and error in my own life.

The tips below are what I've learned so far. But the most important thing to know is this—a healthy, beautiful marriage is possible. It's possible for you, regardless of what happened in your family. Take heart and know that love that lasts is within reach.

A prerequisite to building love that lasts is following Christ's teachings on sexuality. It might strike you as odd, but living a life of purity before marriage is an essential step in making love last within marriage. To learn more about the virtue of chastity, why living together before marriage increases your odds of getting divorced, and why the Church teaches what it does about contraception, go to Chastity.com. Jason Evert's book, *If You Really Loved Me: 100 Questions on Dating, Relationships, and Sexual Purity*, is an excellent resource to answer those questions. His podcast and other content are very helpful as well. Those principles are the starting point, like the foundation of a new home. Naturally, there is more to build above the surface.

First, build virtue. If you want a great marriage, it starts with you. It has nothing to do with your relationship. Why? It's simple. You, and eventually your spouse, are the foundation of your marriage. Your marriage will only be as happy, healthy, and holy as each of you are individually. From the great marriages I've seen, I've learned this undeniable truth: the more virtuous the spouses, the happier the marriage. Always.

Second, find a virtuous spouse. It's not enough to find someone who likes the things you do, who's attractive, or even one who is merely Catholic. They must be virtuous—a person with good habits and a desire to do what is good and avoid what is evil. Why is it so important? For the same reasons above. It truly determines the quality and happiness of your own marriage. A few questions to help you determine if your potential spouse is virtuous:

- Do they have self-mastery, to the point where they can consistently sacrifice what they want in order to do what's best for you?
- Are they living a life of purity, actively uprooting lust where it appears?
- Are they humble, able to apologize and forgive?
- Do they have the ability to see things through your eyes and change their mind?
- Are they actively growing, overcoming their vices and building virtue?
- Is your friendship real and deep?
- Do you want your children to be like them?

Don't try to determine this alone. St. John Paul II said that, as a rule, everyone exaggerates the goodness of the person they love.[42] Make sure you have people who can help you stay objective. Ask yourself, is this person *actually* virtuous? Love is blinding, so involve your friends and mentors—your parents and family if possible, too. Most of all, find someone who puts God first in their life. Listen to the advice of Curtis Martin who said, "Don't pursue your soulmate. Pursue God. After a while of running after him, turn to see who's keeping up."

Third, purify your idea of love. According to Drs. Les and Leslie Parrot, marriage research shows that an essential ingredient for a great marriage is a realistic concept of love.[43] This means knowing the truth about love. This is harder than it sounds, because as a culture, we've been fed lies about love. In order to purify your concept of love, you need to identify those lies and learn the truth that disproves them. One lie that I subconsciously believed is that feelings equal love. Deep down, I believed that feelings were the measure of love. More feeling, more love. Less feeling, less love. And so, in my relationships when feelings would change or fade, I would become anxious. Was love ending? In time, I realized that this wasn't true. I learned that "Love is not merely a feeling; it is an act of will that consists of preferring, in a constant manner, the good of others to the good of oneself."[44] In other words, feelings are a part of love, but they're only a part. And they're certainly not the measure of authentic love.

Fourth, set healthy expectations for your marriage. Again, according to the research, this is another essential ingredient for a great marriage.[45] Often people like us fall into two categories when it comes to marriage: 1) We avoid it to ensure we never repeat our parents' mistakes, or 2) We desire so much the opposite of what our parents had that we develop unrealistic expectations and idolize marriage. I've fallen into the second category. An unhealthy expectation I had was the belief that the purpose of marriage is happiness. I've learned the truth that the purpose of marriage is not happiness. The purpose of marriage is holiness. Nowhere in the wedding vows is happiness promised. This is so important because underneath almost every divorce is this belief: Consciously or not, we expect our spouse to make us perfectly happy. When they don't, we begin to doubt. Did I marry the wrong person? Choose the wrong vocation? We might even be tempted to quit. And so, your marriage will suffer to the extent that you expect your spouse to make you perfectly happy. Does that mean there is no place for happiness in marriage? No! There absolutely is. It's such a good and beautiful thing to make your spouse happy. But marriage takes hard work which involves sacrifice, just like getting in shape, doing well in school, or excelling in your career. It doesn't come easy. Expect it to be challenging, so you won't be surprised when it is. Marriage will be just like life, full of joy and challenges, beauty and frustrations. Why do we expect it to be so different from other parts of our life?

Fifth, learn to handle conflict. You can't have intimacy without conflict. It's impossible. In fact, experiencing no conflict in your marriage is usually a bad sign. The goal is to make conflict healthy. Dr. John Gottman and his team of researchers have discovered that how a couple handles conflict determines the success or failure of their relationship. Supposedly, they can predict with approximately 95% accuracy whether married couples will stay together or break apart by studying how they handle conflict. They determined there are four signs that typically happen in this sequence when marriages fall apart, which Dr. Gottman calls the "Four Horsemen of the Apocalypse":

1. Criticism
2. Contempt
3. Defensiveness
4. Stonewalling

In *Saving Your Marriage Before It Starts,* the authors explain each sign.[46] **Criticism** is any negative comments or actions that attack a person. It differs from complaining, which they define as focused on critiquing actions and not attacking a person. **Contempt** is similar to criticism, but different. It is the intention to harm and psychologically abuse your partner. Signs of contempt are name-calling, sarcasm, and mockery. **Defensiveness** is the result of the former two signs. When we feel attacked, we naturally defend ourselves. Signs of defensiveness include blaming, making excuses, and an unwillingness to take responsibility. **Stonewalling** is emotionally avoiding your spouse. It looks like shutting down emotionally and becoming somewhat unresponsive. These four signs do not mean your marriage is doomed, but that it is heading onto a dangerous course. If these four things become habits, then you are likely headed off a cliff. You need professional help right away. There is a better way to handle conflict. For practical tips on handling conflict, see page 122.

Sixth, love your spouse how they want to be loved. You've likely heard of the five love languages. Dr. Gary Chapman discovered them after working with hundreds of couples. He noticed that some people wanted to be loved in certain ways, but others wanted to be loved in very different ways. He explains that inside each of us is an emotional love tank. When that tank is full, we feel loved. When it is empty, we feel unloved or rejected. When problems occur in relationships, typically it is because that love tank is empty. And so, the goal is to keep your significant other's love tank full and teach him or her how to fill yours. The best tool for that is the five love languages: words of affirmation, acts of service, gifts, quality time, and physical touch. Learn your significant other's love languages and start loving him or her accordingly, even if it isn't second nature for you. To learn more about the five love languages, go to 5lovelanguages.com. Additionally, you can listen to the marriage talk found in the bonus material at the end of this book, which gives an overview of the five love languages. The five love languages will help you build a happier, healthier, and more intimate relationship.

Seventh, make things go right, don't just fix things that go wrong. Early in marriage, my wife and I went to marriage counseling. We were struggling to handle conflict well. Upon starting, I expected the counselor to give us tactics to resolve conflict, but that's not what he did. Instead, he asked us about the overall health of our marriage. He wanted to know how often we were going on dates, having fun together, and having good conversations. In other words, he wasn't interested in merely treating the symptoms but rather the underlying root causes. It reminded me of a principle in the book, *The Anatomy of Peace*. The authors say that we have to spend more time and energy making things go right than fixing things that go wrong.[47] In other words, we need to keep our bodies healthy instead of just fixing them when they become sick. We need to take preventive care of our vehicle instead of waiting for something to go wrong. The lesson is simple, but difficult to live because it involves discipline. It involves winning small daily battles. Some practical ways to do that with your relationship:

- Pray together
- Play together
- Go on weekly dates
- Talk about and make sure you agree about these four important things: God, money, parenting, and handling in-laws

- Talk about sexual intimacy in marriage. A great book to guide those conversations is *Holy Sex! A Catholic Guide to Toe-curling, Mind-blowing, Infallible Loving* by Dr. Gregory Popcak.

You can build a great marriage. Even if you're doubtful because of the example you saw from your parents, it doesn't disqualify you from love. You are capable of building love that lasts. Rely on God's grace more than your own strength and never give up. Keep fighting for your marriage, even when you are tempted to quit. When things get difficult, rely on mentors, counselors, and good friends to help you and your spouse persevere. Don't hesitate to get help sooner rather than later. You will be glad you did. But rest assured that building love that lasts isn't a complete mystery. Follow the tips above and the result will be a happy, healthy, and holy marriage. To get more guidance on building a great marriage, listen to the marriage talk in the bonus material at RestoredMinistry.com/bonus.

QUESTION 18

How do I overcome my fear of love, relationships, and intimacy?

Sitting in a coffee shop in downtown Pittsburgh, I overheard two female friends talking. Their conversation revolved around a boy. Apparently, this guy wanted nothing to do with love and relationships. Although these girls were his friends, they couldn't understand his fear of love and relationships. While I don't know why that guy felt that way, it reminded me of how much I've struggled with a fear of love and intimacy, which has made it hard to trust the women I've dated and even my own wife.

Why was I afraid of love and intimacy? I feared repeating my parents' mistakes, feared that love just wouldn't last, and feared that someone would love me for a time and then abandon me. If I felt destined to repeat the dysfunction I saw in my family, why would I start a family of my own? I knew how painful that experience was for me. I never wanted to put myself through it again, and definitely did not want to put my children through it.

At the root of these fears is the fact that I never learned how to build love that lasts. More than from anyone else, I learned about love and marriage from my parents. Since their example wasn't a good one, I have had to overcome what was deeply ingrained in me.

In relationships, fear and anxiety took over. In my first serious relationship, I was afraid to open up and be vulnerable. I feared that if she saw how broken I was, she wouldn't want me. And so, I loved at arm's length. I didn't let her in. At one point, we only talked about once a week. Eventually, we broke up. I'm convinced that my fear killed the relationship. In my next relationship, I was afraid to even ask her out. Fear controlled me. Again, once I finally asked her to be my girlfriend, I struggled to let her in—though I did learn from the first relationship. If you also struggle to overcome your fear of love and intimacy, here are five tips to help you.

First, accept the risk. Vulnerability is a requirement for authentic love. There's no way around it. It's true that you might get hurt. But do you know what's actually worse? Never loving at all. Speaking about this, C.S. Lewis said it best:[48]

"To love at all is to be vulnerable.
Love anything and your heart will be wrung and possibly broken.
If you want to make sure of keeping it intact you must give it to no one,
not even an animal.
Wrap it carefully round with hobbies and little luxuries;
avoid all entanglements.
Lock it up safe in the casket or coffin of your selfishness.
But in that casket, safe, dark, motionless, airless, it will change.
It will not be broken; it will become unbreakable, impenetrable, irredeemable."

The hard truth is that love almost always involves risk and pain. There's no way to avoid that, as mentioned in *Downton Abbey*, "There's no such thing as safe love. Real love gives someone the power to hurt you," and trusting they won't do it, at least not seriously.[49] But love is worth the risk. To experience the potential happiness, you have to risk the potential hurt. If you work at it, the good outweighs the bad. Your life won't be easier, but it will be better.

Second, do it scared. It's okay to feel afraid. It's

natural. But you can choose to love in spite of your fear. You can choose not to allow fear to control you. Courage doesn't mean never feeling afraid, but rather acting even when you are afraid. Face your fear head-on. Identify it and name it. Write it down or talk to someone about it. Inside our heads, fear is big and loud. When we get it out, we see that it isn't as big or scary as we thought. Then, take action. Say yes to that date. Be vulnerable with your significant other. Action is the antidote to fear. Do it scared.

Third, start confronting your fear in good friendships. It's typically easier to practice vulnerability with friends we've known and trusted for years than a boyfriend or girlfriend. Open up to them over time. Tell them things you are afraid to say. Don't do it all at once or with just anyone. Choose good, trustworthy friends. Then, little by little, begin to open up about your struggles, regrets, brokenness, past mistakes, and your family situation. By doing that, you'll build that vulnerability muscle, so you can better love in romantic relationships.

Fourth, go into romance gradually. People like us typically have to go slower. That's okay. Don't be ashamed, it's normal for people from broken homes. It's typically not wise to dive headfirst into a romantic relationship. Like a plant, relationships need to grow naturally over time. If we try to make them grow too fast, they die. Build a friendship first with your potential mate if you can. You can continue to work on that friendship within your dating relationship, but it's ideal to start that process before you start dating. Patience will solidify trust, which will make your love more beautiful.

Though I've mastered some of my fear, my battle is far from over. Sometimes I win, other times I lose. Through it all, there's a truth that I've learned: **I never regret facing my fears.** On the other hand, I have regretted being controlled by them. Fear is crippling. You feel stuck. To move beyond it, you must walk through it. There's no way around it. But when you move past fear, you are free. In this case, free to love.

In time, I learned to overcome that fear. Feeling afraid, I still pursued my beautiful wife during our senior year of college. After graduation, we dated long-distance for a year. Then, I rented an apartment near her in Philadelphia to date more seriously. Eventually, I asked her to marry me and become my life's companion. On an April afternoon, we got married. We saved up and went to

Europe for our honeymoon, which was incredible. Now, we're building our family. In fact, we recently had our baby girl, Lucy. Words can't describe how much we love her. We hope to continue building our family and making our children feel loved, wanted, and enough.

It's humbling and even overwhelming to realize that I was once so paralyzed by fear and now, I am where I am. I would have never believed it could happen. But it did. You can do it, too. To hear more advice about overcoming your fear of love and intimacy, listen to this Restored podcast episode: RestoredMinistry.com/17.

QUESTION 19

What can I do to get past the barriers that hold me back in love and relationships?

Perhaps the most powerful barrier in pursuing love is the belief that love, or relationships as a whole, won't last. The fear that sooner or later, no matter how good it might be now, it will fall apart. Subconsciously, I believed this at my core. Seeing my parents' marriage end, seemingly out of the blue, I reasoned that love, including friendship love, didn't last. Maybe it could for others, but I doubted it could last for me.

Even though I once felt that fear so strongly, my story thankfully didn't end there. In time, I learned that although love and marriage can fall apart, it can also be so good and beautiful. What convinced me? Spending time with great married couples. There were two beautiful married couples in particular that helped me to believe in love again. They showed me that with hard work and virtue, love can last—not only last, but be so lifegiving and inspiring. Seeing them, I knew I wanted my marriage to be like theirs. Their examples have been very healing for me.

I recommend the same solution to you. Look around. What married couples do you know that have a beautiful marriage? If marriage doesn't seem like an option for you, what individuals do you see that model healthy friendships vibrantly and vulnerably? Develop a relationship with them. Ask the married couples questions about their marriage. Eventually, you can even tell them that because you come from a broken home, you doubt that love can last and that their example is really helpful.

It's also important to remember that love is a choice. It's choosing what's best for the person you love. Thankfully, that choice does not need to be dictated by whatever you are feeling at the moment. You can choose to love God and others regardless of how you feel.

Another belief I held was that sooner or later, my spouse will leave me. I've felt this fear strongly in my own marriage. Because my parents' breakup was so unexpected, I've feared that disaster could be around every corner. As a result, I tend to be very vigilant. As a happily married man, I have no logical reason to think my wife would cheat on me or abandon me. She is a good, beautiful, and faithful woman. But the doubt still sits in the back of my mind. This is dangerous because we tend to act in a way that anticipates their leaving, which plays a role in making it a reality. If you also have this fear, you need to choose a spouse that is good and virtuous. Then, trust they won't abandon you. This can take a while, so be open with your partner about your struggle to trust—in time, their steadfast love will help heal you. It helps a lot if they can remind you that they're not going anywhere.

Lastly, the tendency to settle is a common struggle. Often, people like us are tempted to use a single criteria to choose a spouse—someone who won't leave. It's a recipe for disaster, but unfortunately, it's not uncommon. After all, we just want to feel safe and loved, even if the person isn't right for us. Don't fall for this. Instead, find a virtuous spouse who inspires you to grow. For great advice about how to find your future husband, buy Jason Evert's book, *How to Find Your Soulmate Without Losing Your Soul: 21 Secrets for Women.* To learn how to pursue your wife, buy Jason Evert's book, *The Dating Blueprint: What She Wants You to Know About Dating But Will Never Tell You.* If you want to learn more about healthy intimacy in friendships, check out *The Four Loves* by C.S. Lewis and *Fill These Hearts* by Christopher West.

QUESTION 20

I hate conflict. How do I stop being afraid and handle it better?

In *Primal Loss*, author Leila Miller mentions that children from broken homes learn that conflict leads to permanent separation. After all, conflict led to the breakdown of our families. Having witnessed that, we naturally feel ill-equipped to resolve conflict in our own lives, especially in our romantic relationships. As a result, we typically avoid it altogether. If we can't avoid it, we handle it poorly—just like our parents. This happens the most in marriage, when disagreements are inevitable. Thankfully, all is not lost. We can learn to handle conflict well.

When dealing with conflict, business practitioners teach to always lead with your intention. When you're having a difficult conversation, don't assume the other person knows your intentions. Be clear upfront about why you're bringing up the topic and what you hope to accomplish (e.g. solving a problem, resolving a conflict, strengthening your relationship with them). Hopefully, your intention aligns with what the other person wants, too. Leading with your intention usually prevents a defensive response. For example, you can say, "I want to talk about something that hurt the other day. I'm not trying to accuse, I just want you to understand what I felt and resolve this together."

Next, get straight to the point if you have a good relationship with the person. If not, or if the person is sensitive or prone to defensiveness, start with some form of affirmation. Let them know the good you see in them. Then, clearly and kindly tell them the issue. Don't just focus on "what" but also the "why" behind it. Explain the true impact of their behavior, opinion, or whatever is at the core of the conflict. Then, finish with another affirmation, such as "I've always admired how selfless you are."

Justice for All is a non-profit that teaches people how to have conversations with other people about the hot topic of abortion. They teach that whenever you're discussing a sensitive or difficult topic, such as abortion, use these 3 steps: 1) Ask good questions, 2) Really listen to reflect, not just respond or refute, and 3) Build common ground by finding things you agree upon, so you can proceed to the things you disagree upon.[50]

Next, when sharing how something hurt you, use the phrase "I feel" or "I felt." Avoid the temptation to say "you" or anything that feels accusatory. Again, it disarms the other person so they don't feel attacked. You're simply sharing how what they did made you feel.

Another disarming tactic in heated conversations is saying "You're right" or "I agree." It deflates their anger and usually stops them in their tracks. What if you can't totally agree with them? Find something that you can agree upon within what they're saying, even if it is small. It will help to build common ground.

Some level of vulnerability is necessary in resolving conflict. It's really difficult for someone to understand why you were hurt if you are completely closed off. The more intimate the relationship, the more vulnerable you should be. For less intimate conflicts, only reveal what's necessary to help them understand. It's not always appropriate to tell them your whole life story. A basic understanding and some examples of how it triggered you is enough.

When it's too difficult to face someone in person, write them a letter. When you write it, use the tips above. After finishing it, wait a few days to send it. Reread it to make sure it says everything you want to say in a tone that invites the other person to come alongside you to solve the problem together. If it needs changes, rewrite it. If it looks good, deliver it.

In conflict, it's important that we take the posture of a team that's working together to solve a problem. Blame and accusations will just alienate, make people defensive, and push them away.

A few tips on conflict resolution from the book *Saving Your Marriage Before It Starts*:[51]

- Pick your battles. Learn to let the small things go.
- Practice empathy, placing yourself in another person's shoes by detaching from your emotions and feeling what they do. Repeat what the other person is saying to make sure you really understand their point of view.
- Define the real issue. Often, the issue you are fighting about is not the real problem.
- Take a break. When emotions get heightened, our marriage counselor suggested a timeout from 15 minutes to 24 hours—a time agreed upon outside of conflict. The person who asks for the timeout tracks time and resumes the conversation.

- Use this sentence formula to stay focused on the issue without attacking the person: "In situation X, when you do Y, I feel Z." For example, "The other day, when you worked all day and didn't talk to me, I felt ignored."
- Rate the intensity of your feelings about the issue on a 1–10 scale. One means the issue is not important to you. Ten means there is nothing more important to you. Communicate your number, so it's clear how serious the conflict is.

Most importantly, build trust in your relationships before any conflict occurs. Trust is built in two ways: 1) Consistency and 2) Vulnerability. Consistency means doing what you say you will, again and again. Vulnerability means sharing your weaknesses and allowing someone to see you without a mask on. When trust is high, conflict is either avoided or made healthy. Author Pat Lencioni wrote, "Trust makes conflict the pursuit of truth." In other words, when trust is high, conflict simply becomes a path to reach the best possible solution—not a battle of egos.

Conflict can certainly drive two people further apart. But if you handle it well, do your best to make it healthy, and successfully resolve it, it can actually bring you closer together. If that sounds foreign, it's okay. It usually does to people like us. But when handled respectfully using the tactics above, the solution reached is better and it can even strengthen your relationships. Next time a conflict-ridden situation occurs, put these tactics into action.

QUESTION 21

I tend to be controlling in life and relationships. How can I overcome that tendency?

Trauma survivors tend to desire control in life. Why? Because traumatic events are chaotic and painful. In order to avoid experiencing that again, you seek safety and security at all costs. You think that the best way to achieve that is by controlling everything you can in life, both yourself and other people. It becomes so second nature that you barely notice it.

Underneath a desire for control is often terror or dread. You feel like nobody has your back. Since there is no safety net, you can't screw up. If you do, you feel that all is lost. Control feels like the only viable option, which can lead to perfectionism. You try to do things perfectly in an attempt to prevent mistakes or bad things from happening. Stubbornness is another way the desire to control manifests itself. The attitude that you are not wrong or won't change your mind. But the destination of perfectionism and stubbornness is selfishness and misery.

In my life, I eventually realized that my desire for control in life and in relationships was extremely high. In my first serious relationship, I even tried to control my feelings. I became very anxious when I didn't feel a certain way. It was exhausting, to say the least. Thankfully, I made progress in overcoming my desire for control. It's still there, but it doesn't have the power over me that it once had. If a "Type A" person like me learned to let go, you can too.

Not all control is bad. Self-control is a wonderful thing. Your ability to be disciplined is extremely admirable. But we have to recognize our limits. We have to "control the controllables," and accept the rest.

How do you overcome your excessive desire for control? Start by uncovering why you want control. Most likely, your story has specific events or themes that triggered your desire for control. Once you understand the root cause, you'll be better equipped to find the correct countermeasure.

Increase your tolerance for powerlessness, helplessness, and loss of control. It will be a recurring feeling throughout your life, whether due to life circumstances, accidents, illness, relationship shifts, or other things. View the moments where you can connect to, tolerate, and accept your feelings that feel intolerable as moments where you are growing. Think of it as expanding your window of tolerance for emotions that are difficult to endure. Breath deeply and trust that you will be okay. Powerlessness will not kill you, but it certainly triggers old wounds. Those wounds, festering beneath the surface, can do real harm if we don't connect to our feelings and expand our capacity to receive them with acceptance.

Be selfless by taking a step back. Instead of only thinking of yourself and what you want, let other people have their way—assuming that what they want is good. Genuinely listen to what they think. Practice letting other people choose by giving in to their preference in small decisions like where to eat or what movie to watch.

Similarly, be a follower. Being a leader is good. Perhaps you even excel in that role. But take a backseat from time to time. It might make you feel uneasy, but it will help you grow. Get comfortable not being in control. In situations where you may think that you could do a better job, don't automatically take charge. Just because you might be more competent doesn't mean you need to take control.

Remember that in your relationships, you can't prevent every mistake. Sometimes, you have to let people fail. You are not responsible for other people's choices. Unless the failure is fatal, it's usually a very effective teacher. Many people won't learn a lesson until they make a mistake.

Ask yourself: Has controlling everything in your life always prevented bad things from happening? You'll discover it has not. And worse, it usually prevents you from experiencing a lot of good and beautiful things in life because you are so busy controlling everything.

Keep in mind that your value doesn't come from your perfectionism. It doesn't come from your lack of mistakes. Your value is rooted in the fact that you are a unique, unrepeatable, irreplaceable human person created and loved by God. That's it. All your qualities and accomplishments are a bonus.

Being a controlling person will only damage your relationships. People hate being controlled and may pull away from you as a result. But if you learn to let go and stop trying to control people and things, while retaining proper control over yourself and your responsibilities in life, you'll build better relationships. You'll feel more free. You'll experience more peace. Control the controllables and surrender the rest to God.

QUESTION 22

How do I stop relying on people, like a girlfriend or boyfriend, in an unhealthy way?

When you feel broken and alone, it's natural to look for someone to help you. But often, it's very easy to bring the pain and problems to people who aren't equipped to help you solve them, such as a friend, boyfriend, or girlfriend. You may develop an unhealthy reliance on them, which ends up hurting the relationship, the other person, and you, too. Naturally, a marriage relationship looks different than a friendship or dating relationship, which is the focus here.

How do you know if you have an unhealthy reliance on another person (often called a codependent relationship)? A few signs:

- Every move of that person affects you greatly. Your life feels like an emotional roller coaster.
- Your relationship is a crutch that holds you, or

both of you, up. If the relationship were to end, you'd feel lost.
- You feel unstable without him or her, like life doesn't make sense. While it's okay to miss someone and to be thrown off when that person is not in your life, it shouldn't feel almost impossible to keep living.

In high school, I tried to help female friends of mine who were struggling. Those relationships became unhealthy. In one case my friend had real problems, so I wanted to solve them for her. This created an unhealthy one-way friendship, where I invested heavily to help her out temporarily. Eventually, I knew something needed to change. I told her the relationship didn't feel right and we needed to take a step back. We remained friends, but changed the way we interacted. It helped a ton.

In my dating relationships, I became overly dependent on my first girlfriend. The condition of our relationship affected me so much. I obsessed over it. When it was good, I was good. When it was bad, I seriously struggled. Eventually I learned that a balance is needed between togetherness and separateness. Utter dependence on another person isn't healthy, but neither is a rigorous independence. There is a middle ground.

Psychologists say that a healthy relationship looks like the letter "M."[52] Imagine two people standing side by side, with hands joining to form an "M." That represents a healthy interdependence, which is the balance between personal independence and healthy dependence on others—the ideal relationship. If one person left the relationship, their absence would be felt but it would not destroy the other person. Opposite this balanced approach on both ends of the spectrum are unhealthy dependence, represented by the letter "A," and unhealthy independence, signified by the letter "H." In an unhealthy dependence, each partner is overly reliant on the other person for their happiness and well-being. The letter "A" signifies two people leaning heavily on each other. If one person left the relationship, the other person would be debilitated. In an unhealthy independence, both partners are so separate that they are barely affected by the relationship. The letter "H" signifies two people who barely connect or rely on each other. If one person left, the partner would barely notice it.

What letter would you use to rate your own romantic relationship, or even your close friendships: M, A, or H? Given the answer, you'll know what to do. If the relationship is balanced ("M"), no change is needed. Simply maintain what you've built. If the relationship is overly dependent ("A"), then you need to create more space and independence in the relationship. If the relationship is overly independent ("H"), then you need to form a closer bond, practice vulnerability, and begin to form a healthy reliance on the other person.

At the core of an interdependent relationship is healthy detachment. Healthy detachment is the ability to remain separate and not overly attached to a person, so that you retain your individuality while at the same time having a proper attachment to the person and experiencing togetherness. You need to learn to stand on your own two feet. It's healthy. It's good for you. Not to the point where you feel that you don't need anyone, but to the point where you aren't wrecked by your relationship problems. It's the attitude of "I don't need you, but I want you in my life. I choose you, not out of desperation but out of love."

In romantic relationships, the strength of your long-term attraction is dependent upon this dynamic. Attraction is strongest when there is a natural distance between two people. If too far apart, attraction dies. If too close together, attraction also dies. That middle ground of togetherness and separateness is a tricky balance. But it is at the core of what keeps the strong draw that two people feel toward each other, like two magnets whose attraction is strongest at a slight distance. When pulled further apart, the magnetic pull is gone. When so close together, the attraction ceases too. Attraction requires space.

Overall, space is healthy in a relationship. Like the flame of a bonfire, a relationship requires space to breathe and grow. If you smother it, it will die. And so, let your relationship grow naturally. Don't be afraid to spend time apart. During that time apart, understand that you're investing in your relationship. On the opposite hand, don't allow your fierce independence to prevent you from emotionally investing in your relationship.

In order to fix an imbalance in your relationship, do three things: First, identify the imbalance. You might need help from a mentor to do so. Tell them the details of your relationship. Be brutally honest. Ask their feedback and assessment about whether the relationship is unhealthy.

Second, call out the unhealthy balance. Talk about it with the other person in the relationship.

Share what you've learned and how you've seen your relationship with them shift into an unhealthy zone. Say that because you want the relationship to last and be healthy, changes are needed. If you're the one who is relying heavily on the other person, tell them what concrete actions you will take to pull away a bit (e.g. not texting or calling as frequently, turning to older mentors about your problems before discussing with your significant other, and so on).

Third, commit to concrete actions to form a healthy relationship. Brainstorm ideas together for what you can do to make the relationship healthy and balanced. That might involve avoiding heavy topics together or spending more time with groups of friends instead of one-on-one.

While all of this naturally applies in romantic relationships, it applies in other relationships too: friends, siblings, and parents. Don't be afraid to end a relationship or take a break if the relationship is very unhealthy. That might be the action needed for both of you. That break will help you to determine the condition of your relationship (whether it's an M, A, or H relationship) and create a plan to heal it.

While an unhealthy reliance on another person might feel good in the moment, it will only leave you feeling more desperate. You'll feel like you can't survive without that person to the point where you seriously struggle if things in the relationship aren't good. Your need for constant reassurance in the relationship will hold you and your partner back.

If you find yourself there, don't despair. You can learn how to hit the balance of interdependence. Start making the adjustments needed in your relationship this week.

Healing Tactics to Help You Feel Whole Again

QUESTION 23

What is grieving and how does it work?

Grief is the process by which you come to accept a loss. In other words, it's a series of steps you take to make peace with the reality of losing someone or something. It is not easy, but it is a natural reaction that you experience during a loss, and it's how you learn to live with it.

The loss doesn't have to be catastrophic to be worthy of grieving. It can look like losing your pet, your best friend moving away, or losing your car from an accident. It can be more serious too, such as losing a friend or family member to death, or your family breaking apart because of your parents' divorce. Despite what some people say, your parents' divorce or separation is a serious loss. It's incredibly important to admit this loss and to give yourself the space to grieve your parents' divorce. This is one of the essential parts to feeling whole again. Even though there may be pressure from friends and family to be happy and to move on, you need to honor yourself by processing this trauma.

Traditionally, grieving has five steps or phases, which you've probably heard before:

- Denial
- Sadness
- Bargaining
- Anger
- Acceptance

It's important to note that these steps don't always happen in order. Step one and step five typically happen first and last, but the others can vary. Furthermore, it's not unusual to revisit the various steps. The process is messy. Some steps might even overlap. To illustrate each step, I'll share my experience of grieving the loss of a family member who committed suicide.

Denial is the disbelief you feel when learning about the loss. My dad approached me as I worked at my desk. I saw his face was covered in tears. Immediately, I stepped away from my computer. "What's wrong?" I said, worried. He explained that a relative had killed himself. I reacted by saying, "No, that's not possible." I couldn't believe it was real. I didn't want it to be real.

Sadness is a feeling you have when you begin to grasp the reality of the situation. It quickly occurred for me. Initially, I hugged my dad to console him. Once he left, I began crying harder than I had in years. It hit me hard. The sadness of the situation overcame me.

Bargaining is an odd word, but it means thinking about all the ways in which you felt like you could have prevented the loss. With my relative, I immediately felt guilty for losing contact with him that summer. I thought, "If only I could've been there for him, perhaps he would not have killed himself." As convincing as it can seem, the truth is that bargaining is often a futile attempt to reverse a painful reality. It's an attempt to feel some sort of control amidst chaos.

Anger is often what you feel when you realize the wrongness or injustice of the situation. In the aftermath of my relative's death, I felt anger toward him. How could he be so selfish? Didn't he know how much it would hurt us? How could he think we'd be better off without him? Though you don't always feel anger toward the person you lost, it's not unusual. In some cases, your anger might be directed toward someone else, such as a doctor, family member, yourself, or God.

Acceptance is the resolution. Although the loss hurts, you've come to understand that you can't undo it. You can't go back in time and prevent it. The only option is to come to terms with this new reality. The fruit of that acceptance is peace. While the previous steps indicate struggle or disturbance, acceptance means finally admitting the truth: The loss was painful and mattered, but it cannot be undone. It means taking the painful loss and accepting it as part of your story. I don't know why, but acceptance happened rather quickly for me. Unlike some family members, I seemed to move through the grieving steps quicker. At that point, I knew the best I could do was to love my family in the pain and pray for my relative's soul.

Not everyone grieves at the same pace. Some people move more quickly than others. You might even process various losses differently. That's okay. There's no exact formula. The worst thing you can do during grieving is to stop yourself from feeling your feelings—to shove them away or distract yourself. Don't do that. Sit there, in the grief. Allow yourself time. It's okay not to be okay. It's also detrimental to stay isolated. Naturally, you likely want to be alone. Give yourself space. But don't stay alone for long. Allow someone to be there with you in your pain. The most healing and helpful thing is not someone who makes it all better or tells you to look on the bright side. But rather, someone who can just be there with you and feel the pain with you. In fact, "look on the bright side" is bad advice when you're grieving. Feel your feelings and trust that in time, you will come out the other side.

Similar to my relative's death, my parents' separation and divorce was a serious loss in my life. Immediately, I denied it was possible for my parents to break apart. Sure, things at home weren't perfect, but we were a family. In that situation, I felt sadness right away too. I hid in the closet and cried. For months after, that sadness still remained, though it quickly turned to anger. I hated everyone involved in the breakup, especially my dad and mom. With anger also came bargaining, thinking that I could have prevented my parents' breakup had I been a better son or had been there for them. Acceptance, in this case, was not nearly as quick as with my relative's suicide. I had a hard time accepting it because this was my own life, and I wanted it to be so different. In time,

I did accept it. But it wasn't easy, because my parents' divorce was treated like a normal, everyday thing—not a trauma. Eventually, I did make peace with the fact that my parents will most likely never be together again. It still hurts, but I have accepted it as part of my story.

Allow yourself to grieve the serious loss of your parents' divorce or separation. Allow yourself to feel your feelings, even the messy ones. It's okay not to be okay. Work toward acceptance at your own pace. It will bring peace and freedom to move on. It will prevent you from staying stuck in the past. It will help you function normally again. It doesn't mean you'll never hurt again. It doesn't mean that the trauma is completely healed, but it does mean that you've dealt with it for now, so you can keep going in spite of the loss.

QUESTION 24

I feel broken, like something is wrong with me. How can I heal and feel whole again?

Healing is the process of becoming healthy and whole, especially after a wound or trauma. You know what this looks like physically. If you broke your arm, it would be painful. You'd go to the hospital. The doctor would examine your arm to understand the injury. Most likely, he would take an X-ray to give him a better picture of the wound. You may be given pain medication. From there, surgery might be necessary. Your arm would be placed in a cast. After some period of time, you would go to physical therapy. Through therapy, you would regain function in your arm, hopefully to the point of it becoming healthy and whole again.

Healing needs to happen for emotional wounds, as well. Nothing illustrates this better than the powerful story of speaker and author Crystalina Evert. Her first memory is of her dad hitting her mom. As a two year old, her father left her and divorce followed soon after. As a young girl, she was sexually abused, only adding to the trauma. As a teenager, she fell into drugs, alcohol, and sleeping around. As a high school sophomore, she started her first serious relationship. Thinking it was love, she gave her virginity to her boyfriend. But in time, he cheated on her. Miserable and alone, she heard a chastity talk. Inspired by the story of the speaker, she began to change her life and save herself for her husband. Life improved so much for her. She met her husband, got married, and had kids. But years later, as a wife and mother, her wounds resurfaced. She felt anger, shame, and a whole host of messy emotions. The worst part was when she let it out on her husband and kids.

One day, she realized that for so long she had just stuffed away her wounds instead of dealing with them. As a result, she was now passing her brokenness onto the people she loved the most. Realizing this, she made a vow: "It stops with me."

She committed herself to healing. She began counseling, found a great spiritual director, and spent countless hours in adoration. She wrote a lot, including letters to the people who harmed her. It was an intense and difficult period for her. By the end of three hard years, she felt different. She felt so free, lighter, and more confident. She was a stronger woman and became a better wife and mother. Amazingly, she was no longer ashamed of her painful past.

That's what healing is meant to do—transform you into a better, stronger, and healthier person. It doesn't mean you'll never suffer again. But it does mean you'll be better able to handle that suffering and find meaning in life.

However, there are two common barriers to healing. First is simply not dedicating the time needed to heal. You may fail to make it a priority because you think, "What's done is done." You don't make the connection between the events in your past and your current struggles. To solve your current struggles, you need to heal from past wounds. Hopefully this book and your desire to feel whole again will convince you that the time and effort to heal are worth it. That you are worth it. But ultimately, only you can choose to put in the work. The second barrier is not knowing how to heal. As a teenager, I felt broken and knew I needed to heal, but I had no clue how to start. If you feel that way, the four tips below offer simple steps.

The first tip: Engage your story. Each of us has a story, like a movie or novel. To engage your story simply means to reflect on it. Reflect on the things that have happened to you and the people involved. The most important part of your story is the people that cared for you during childhood, especially your parents. Reflecting on your story is actually healing on a neurobiological level. It literally makes your brain healthier by increasing neural connectivity, according to therapist Adam Young who hosts the podcast *The Place We Found Ourselves.*[53] Furthermore, he says that sharing your story with another person who is able to receive the story and empathize with you is also incredibly healing on a neurobiological level. To help with all of this, Adam Young suggests naming your wounds. Be very specific, such as "Mom abused me" or "Dad abandoned me." It is harder to clearly identify how you've been harmed than it seems. But it's worth the effort, because "when it comes to experiencing healing, naming how you've been harmed is about 70% of the battle."[54] To explore this type of therapy more, look into Narrative therapy.

The second tip: Write about the emotionally significant events in your life. As a young husband, James Pennebaker and his wife were struggling in their marriage. Both doubted they had made the right decision to get married. He fell into depression and felt very lonely. One day at home, he saw his typewriter and spontaneously started writing about everything that was happening to him. He wrote without holding back and put it all on paper. After doing this for three days, something amazing happened—his depression left him.

As a professor, he spent the next 40 years studying the link between writing and emotional processing. In conducting studies, he would divide people into two groups and tell the first group to write about emotionally significant events in their lives. He instructed the second group to write about everyday things, such as the weather, clothes, or sports. He told both groups to write for 20 minutes a day, four days in a row. The results were astounding. They found that the people who wrote about emotionally significant events in their lives experienced an increase in physical and mental well-being, were happier, less depressed, less anxious, reported higher quality relationships, better memory, more success at work, and much more.[55]

Numerous studies have confirmed the findings. It's clearly worth the time to write about emotionally significant events in your life. In the future, Restored will produce a guided journal specifically for helping people like us from broken homes to walk through healing exercises and more. In the meantime, you can check out Professor James Pennebaker's work by checking out his book, *Expressive Writing: Words That Heal.*

The third tip: Find a coach. I recommend three types of coaches: 1) a counselor, 2) a spiritual director, and 3) a mentor. A counselor is specifically trained to help you engage your story and heal from the trauma in your life. Though the goal of counseling varies with each person, the overall objective is to help you face and heal your wounds, so you can feel whole again and become the best you. Sometimes, that means helping you make sense of the past. Other times, it means learning skills to handle the struggles you're facing right now. A spiritual director's job is to help you discern God's plan for your life, heal your relationship with God, and grow closer to him. Spiritual direction is not counseling and your spiritual director is not a commander who tells you how to live your life. He or she is just meant to help you interpret what God is communicating to you and figure out what to do next to heal your relationship with him. Finally, a mentor is someone wiser who can help you with general guidance in life. While they don't have specific training like counselors or spiritual directors, they have wisdom through experience. They are someone you admire and want to be like. It could be a teacher, coach, friend's parent, or whoever. My mentors have consisted of priests, youth ministers, speakers, and family friends. Typically, it's someone with whom you already have at least a basic relationship. From there, do a trial run by asking them for advice for a specific situation. It might feel intimidating to approach them, but you can say, "I need some guidance on a situation or struggle I'm dealing with. Could I ask for your advice?" Ideally this is face-to-face. But virtually works too. If you want a coach that Restored vets and recommends, go to RestoredMinistry.com/coaching.

The fourth tip to find healing is building good friendships. Psychologist and author Dr. Bob Schuchts teaches that at the root of every wound is a deprivation of love. In other words, your wounds usually happen within your relationships. And so, your healing needs to happen in relationships, too. Healing is not simply a checklist of actions to take. It is very relational. At its core, it involves opening up to a small group of people, allowing them to see you as you actually are, and letting them love you with full knowledge of your brokenness. My friendships have been so helpful in overcoming my feelings of not being enough, unwanted, and abandoned. They've taught me to trust again, too. But there is a limit with people who don't know what it's like to come from a broken family. For that, I recommend finding a few people to whom you can speak openly about your struggles and past. They can empathize with you in ways that people from intact families simply cannot. You can build a community like that on your own or join Restored's private online community at RestoredMinistry.com/community.

Most importantly, in order to heal you have to believe it is possible. If you don't, you won't even try. To believe it, you have to see it in action. Look for people in your life who are thriving, especially people from broken families who have had to work through it. Their stories will inspire you to believe that healing is possible. On our podcast, we have numerous stories exactly like that. To listen, go to RestoredMinistry.com/podcast.

Also, be patient with yourself. Healing doesn't happen overnight. It's a marathon, not a sprint. During that time, focus on the effort and not the outcome. The outcome will happen as a result of the effort. A lot of times you want the outcome right away, but that's not how it works, so keep at it. If you're afraid, that's okay. Healing is scary and intimidating. It is easier not to do it. It takes courage. But remember, courage is not the absence of fear; it is acting in spite of your fear. It means doing it scared.

If you don't heal, you'll continue to feel broken and stuck in life. But if you do heal, you will feel free to navigate the joys and challenges of life with greater ease, resiliency, and peace. Free from anxiety, depression, and loneliness. Free to build love and intimacy. Free to be confident and courageous. Free to be the authentic you. You *can* get there. Countless people have been where you are. They've taken the path of healing and reached the summit. You can become the person you desire to be, the person you were born to be. You can have the life you deeply desire. It's not a privilege for a few, but a real possibility for everyone. It doesn't mean you'll never struggle or suffer again. But you will become better and more virtuous. You will experience the happiness and freedom for which you were made.

QUESTION 25

What is a victim mentality and how do I beat it?

Over the years, I've found so much healing. But it didn't happen right away. I wasted a lot of time feeling sorry for myself. I wasted a lot of time wishing things were different, but not doing anything to change them. I wasted a lot of time blaming my parents—especially my dad—for the pain and problems in my life instead of taking responsibility to solve them. In short, I fell into a "victim mentality."

So many of us fall into a victim mentality—the mindset that refuses to take responsibility for our wounds and problems in our lives, even though we've had the opportunity to do so. There are two core beliefs underneath this mentality: 1) We believe our wounds from the past and problems in the present determine our identity and future, and 2) We believe we're powerless, that there is nothing we can do to heal our wounds and solve our problems.

Why do we choose to remain victims? There are many reasons, but here are a few: 1) It's comfortable because it's what we know, 2) Healing is painful and difficult, and 3) We fear that if our brokenness no longer existed, we'd be abandoned by the people whose attention it captured. If we stopped being broken, would they still be there for us?

Remaining a victim leaves us feeling stuck and helpless. Stuck as spectators in our lives, like we have no say or control. Helpless as we feel like life will always be this broken. We perpetually wait for someone to rescue us, to ease our pain, and solve our problems—without much effort from us. Often, it causes us to form unhealthy relationships with a friend or significant other since we desire a rescuer. Is that desire bad? No, but it is harmful to the extent that it leaves us helpless and stuck. It's harmful to the extent that we take our pain and problems to someone who can't give us the help we need, like a friend or significant other.

The truth is that only God can truly rescue us. But even he won't take away our choice. We have to decide to work with him. One man said, "God feeds the birds, but he doesn't throw the worms into the nest."[56] We can't expect him to ignore our free will and do everything for us. He wants us to team up with him and work a way out of victimhood.

Now, naturally people will have objections when reading this. They ask, "What about addiction? Isn't one of the twelve steps admitting that you're powerless over your addiction?" Yes. In addiction, we must admit we're powerless over it. 12-step programs are very helpful and effective. But just because we can't overcome an addiction *on our own*, does not mean we cannot overcome it *at all* with God's help and the help of others. And so, we are not admitting we are so completely powerless that we might as well resign and give into our brokenness. If that were the case, it would be useless to try. Rather, we just can't do it *alone.*

In the book *Boundaries*, the authors say that even in situations of addiction, we do have the power to do some things that will bring control and freedom eventually. Those things include but are certainly not limited to:

- Facing and admitting our problems
- Offering our powerlessness to God
- Asking God and others to help us

Another potential objection is: "But there are certainly real victims." Absolutely. Trauma is real. Children of divorce are truly victims of divorce. Even if the separation was necessary due to abuse or violence, it is still harmful, and loss of the child's family has still occurred. As people who've endured our parents' breakup, we were very much victims.

But we're not meant to remain victims forever. We can simultaneously say: I was harmed, and it will not define me. I refuse to let it hold me back. I refuse to remain a victim. How do we overcome a victim mentality? Here are five tips to do so.

First, identify when you've fallen into a victim mentality. This awareness might sound simple, but it isn't always immediately obvious. It takes time to put your finger on it. Reflect on it. Write about your reflections if it helps. Pray about it. Talk to a friend, mentor, or anyone who knows you well who might be able to point out how you've fallen into a victim mentality. You can even show them this section to prepare them. A sign which may indicate that you've fallen into a victim mentality is an area of your life that either feels stuck or out of control, and when you find yourself thinking or saying, "I can't . . ."

Second, redefine your identity. It's common to hear people addicted to something say, "I am an addict." I understand why. There is power in admitting our problems and powerlessness. It begins the process of overcoming them. But it seems unhealthy to me, because saying "I am an addict" implies an identity instead of conveying an experience or struggle. It is better to say, "I *have* an addiction." The same applies in our case as "children of divorce." I understand why we use that phrase—it is descriptive. But I'm not a fan of the term. Again, it implies an identity instead of describing an experience. Instead of saying "I *am* a child of divorce," it is better to say, "I come from a divorced family" or "my parents are divorced." Because although addiction or our parents' divorce impact who we are greatly, it does not determine our identity or value. St. John Paul II famously wrote: "We are not the sum of our weaknesses and failures, we are the sum of the Father's love for us and our real capacity to become the image of His Son Jesus." Our true identity is that we are beloved creatures of God, or if baptized, sons or daughters of God. You are a unique, irreplaceable, unrepeatable, human being made in God's image and likeness. And so, remind yourself often:

- You are not the sum of the trauma you've experienced.
- You are not the sum of the mistakes you've made.
- You are the sum of God's love for you, seen most clearly on the cross.

Third, change your mindset from victim to hero. Once you've endured trauma, the goal is to shift from victim to survivor and then from survivor to hero. The survivor mindset is that the trauma happened; it hurt and it was real. But it will not define me. It will not control me. It will not write the rest of my life's story. A hero's mindset is different: I will use the bad and painful experiences in my life to thrive, to conquer, to love, and to help other people. To be clear, "hero" doesn't mean superhero, but rather the protagonist in a story. They're usually imperfect and flawed. But they fight for what they want. They take responsibility for the problems in their lives that prevent them from getting what they want. They work hard to overcome them. The difference between a hero and a victim is that the hero is standing on top of their problems instead of being crushed by them. The hero allows his pain and problems to be a catalyst for healing and growth rather than a barrier to it. This is what God wants for us, even in the midst of suffering. Martyrs who've suffered greatly had this hero's mentality even in the midst of great anguish. They were not victims. They were victors or heroes. And so, even in the midst of suffering, we're not meant to remain victims because God can transform even suffering and evil into good.

Fourth, take ownership and action. The divorce wasn't our fault. We weren't to blame. But we do need to take ownership of the brokenness in our lives. We didn't cause the problem, but it is up to us to take ownership of the solution. Nobody can or will do it for us. We have to work to solve problems and heal the wounds in our lives. Take ownership of your life and your problems. Most importantly, take action to make yourself and your life better. The fact that you're reading this book is proof that you're well on your way. Keep going.

Fifth, learn from people who've refused to remain victims. Learning from a mentor in person is ideal, but you can even learn from someone who's not directly in your life—an author, speaker, historical figure, or whomever. Ryan Job is one of those people. He was a real victim. As a Navy SEAL, he fought in Iraq. On patrol one day, he got hit in the face by a sniper's bullet. Luckily, he survived—but he lost his vision. He would never see again. Following that tragic day, Ryan could have been totally debilitated by his wounds. He could have given up, because he was a real victim. He had every reason to remain a victim, but he refused. The wound that cost him his vision did not stop him from living a good and full life. As a blind man, he did incredible things:

- He summited 14,411 foot Mount Rainier, a climb that people have died attempting
- He trained for a triathlon
- He earned his bachelor's degree with a 4.0 GPA
- He successfully hunted an elk
- He married his girlfriend and had a child with her

He could have stayed a victim. He could have felt sorry for himself. But he refused. You can do the same.

Take action on these tips this week. Rely on God's grace more than your own strength through prayer and the sacraments. He will provide for you to the degree that you rely on him. Your scars won't disappear. But with God's help, you can transform your wounds into a source of strength and healing like the nail marks of the risen Jesus. So, trust him greatly. If you do, the result is that you'll get unstuck, start to find real solutions to problems, become a happier and healthier person, and in the end, experience a freedom that's better than any sort of victimhood.

Navigating Your Relationship with Your Parents

QUESTION 26

How do I love and help my parents?

One day, the mom of a fourteen-year-old boy suddenly abandoned her family, never to return. Her departure left his dad so depressed and debilitated that he struggled to function. Wanting to help, the boy dropped out of school and immediately took ownership of the cooking, cleaning, and shopping to compensate for his mother's absence. While most of us wouldn't drop out of school at fourteen, we share this same desire to help our parents. Seeing the problems in their lives and the suffering they experience, we naturally want to help them. However, we might not know how to do it in a healthy way.

First, remember that "people can change, but you can't change them."[57] They have to change themselves. You can influence them, but they must choose to change. If your mom or dad are choosing an unhealthy way of living, realize that you are not responsible for their actions. They are. You cannot change them, they must change themselves.

By far, the best thing you can do is to live a virtuous life—a life of good habits and an internal disposition to do what is good. Live a healthy life in every way possible. Your example is much more likely to inspire change in your parents than the words you say.

Set and enforce healthy boundaries with your parents. This not only helps you but it helps them too. They need to know what is acceptable and what is not acceptable. Boundaries are the lines you draw that tell people what you will and will not allow. When someone breaks a boundary, it must be enforced. It's useless to have boundaries if there are no consequences for breaking them. Boundaries are most needed when it comes to emotionally supporting your parents.

Do not become your mom or dad's primary emotional support. It's unhealthy for you and them, even though it feels like you're helping them. Instead, redirect your parents to people who can properly support them: their family, friends, a mentor, pastor, counselor, and so on. As much as you want to help, it's not your role to be your parent's confidant about their struggles, especially with their spouse. You are their child. You should remain their child, not assume the role of their spouse.

If things get too difficult, dramatic, or toxic, you might need to take a break from that parent who is causing the issues. At one point, I did not approve of my dad's behavior. I didn't like the way he was treating my mom, my siblings, and me. I told him that I wouldn't speak to him until I saw changes in his life. For more than a year, we didn't speak. At one point, I explained in a letter that I wanted a relationship with him, but I wouldn't engage with him until I saw him improve the way he treated everyone. Eventually, he did improve and we resumed our relationship. Sometimes, love must be tough like that. Don't be afraid to take a break. Write a letter if it's helpful. Explain your intentions, but don't expect them to respond well. If they try to bully you or pressure you to go back on your boundary, don't do it. Find a friend or mentor to talk to about whatever you're going through.

In situations where you have become your mom or dad's confidant—the person with whom they share intimate struggles and rely on for their stability and support—tell your parents: "Mom/Dad, I know you're hurting right now. It breaks my heart. I want to help you, but I have to help you in another way. I can't be the person you bring your problems to. Who can you talk to about all of this stuff?" Suggest someone they can confide in. If it gets bad enough, contact that person and let them know you need their help since your parent is relying on you too much.

Unfortunately, it's so common for Mom and Dad to badmouth each other. To say mean things and even divulge secrets or rumors about their spouse. Usually, it's just done out of frustration. Sometimes, it's done in order to turn you against the other parent. If there are details you need to know, a healthy and mature parent can sit you down and calmly tell you what happened. But it's not necessary to continually bring up those things. They might feel like they're at war with their spouse, but that person is still your mom or dad. Tell them that. You can say: "Dad, it really hurts when you say those things about Mom. I know you guys don't like each other, but please remember that she's still my mom. Would you please not talk about her when my siblings and I are around?" If he doesn't respond well, insist that you will not put up with it. Leave the room when he brings up the topic or redirect the conversation. If things get unsafe or dramatic, make sure to call your other parent or an adult you trust and get away.

Another common experience for people like us is being the middleman, the person who relays information between Mom and Dad. This can be extremely stressful and anxiety-provoking. The tricky thing is, you might feel that if you were to step away from this role, your siblings would be forced into it. It doesn't have to be that way. Those aren't the only options. Talk to your mom or dad, or write them a letter. Convey that you are no longer willing to be a middleman. If they want to tell each other something, they have to go through their lawyer, counselor, friend, or family member. Tell them not to use your siblings in your place, as you will not tolerate that, either. You can start by asking nicely, but be firm if they don't comply. There's nothing wrong with being the middleman for simple logistical things like coordinating when Mom or Dad will pick you up for the weekend, but don't feel the temptation to be their negotiator. It's not your job. They are adults, and they need to act like it. Most importantly, talk to your siblings. Make an agreement with them that none of you will be the middleman. You can even tell your parents that you and your siblings are in agreement and will not allow that to happen.

Along with playing the middleman is feeling forced to choose sides. This is called triangulation. Sometimes, Mom or Dad will present you with "evidence" that the other is bad, whether it's true or not. In that situation, you can say a few things. You can acknowledge the issue they are conveying by saying, "Yes, that's definitely wrong." But if they press you further to pick sides, remind them: "Dad, what you said she did is disturbing and wrong, but please remember that you're talking about my mom. How would you react if someone told you that about your mom?" Avoid the pressure to pick sides. Do your best to be diplomatic. In some cases though, it can happen that one spouse is totally in the wrong and to blame for almost everything that happened in the breakdown of the marriage and family. In that case, it's okay to be vocal about what you believe is right. But in time, do your best to let your parents figure that stuff out. You should be their child, nothing more.

While there are plenty of examples of unhealthy ways to help your parents, there are healthy ways too. Usually it's not complicated. Do your chores around the house if you're living at home. If you're a handy or techy person, help them with some home projects or technology. If they need input on minor decisions, feel free to offer it. But major decisions shouldn't be placed on you. That's unfair to ask, so stick to the simple stuff. Never be afraid to say, "I'm sorry, I don't know what to say and I'd prefer not to talk about that. Could you talk to your family or friends about it?"

If it's possible and healthy, spend time with each parent. Build a relationship with them. Do things together. Have good conversations. Ask good questions. Keep things light, especially if they're usually heavy and dramatic. As much as you're able, keep the focus on your relationship with that parent, not the other parent. Allow yourself to be a kid. It's so common to grow up faster than you should as a child of divorce or separation. Savor the moments when you can just be a kid. That's what it's supposed to be like. I am so sorry if your childhood has been hijacked because of your parents' decisions. I know what it's like.

Be honest with how you're feeling. If the parent can't handle your honesty, then make sure you confide in someone else, ideally a mentor. Instead of bottling your feelings inside, get them off your chest. Whether in person or over the phone, communicate with your parents. If the conversation goes south, redirect it with a question or statement (e.g. "Can we talk about something else?" or "I don't want to talk about this right now"). Avoid arguing over text messages. Email is better. Letters are especially helpful. Just make sure that after you write what you feel needs to be said, you let it sit for a day or two to make sure you aren't saying something you'll regret.

The goal for your relationship with your parents is that it is a parent-child relationship. When you are an adult, it can become an adult-to-adult relationship, though they will always be your parents. Resist the temptation to be their savior. That's God's role. Do your best to love and honor your parents in healthy ways, without allowing them or anyone to use or abuse you. In the end, your boundaries and love for your parents will make the relationships healthy, or at least help you avoid a toxic relationship.

QUESTION 27

What can I do to heal my relationship with my parents?

When your parents' marriage breaks apart, it's common for your relationship with one or both parents to fall apart or get damaged in the process. Growing up, I was a "daddy's boy." My father was my hero. When I learned that he was leaving and my parents were pursuing a divorce, it completely shattered my world and my relationship with my dad. It also damaged my relationship with my mom. Over the years, I've tried to heal my relationship with them. It's always a work in progress, but thankfully it's much better now than it used to be.

At the core of healing those relationships is forgiveness. But there's a lot of confusion surrounding the topic of forgiveness. Forgiveness is not simply letting someone off the hook. It's not a feeling. It is not saying what happened didn't hurt or didn't matter. It's freeing someone from the debt that they owe you because they hurt you. Think of it this way: If someone crashes into your car, they have to pay for the damages inflicted on you and your vehicle. That's justice. It's the same way when someone harms you in any other way. You feel they owe you for the damage they did. In justice, they truly do owe you to apologize and compensate you for the damage. Forgiveness releases them of their debt.

There is a process to forgive. It begins with counting the cost. You can make a list that answers these questions: How did my parents harm me? What did they prevent me from having? Which struggles did they directly or indirectly cause? Be detailed and brutally honest. We all have a tendency to protect and defend our parents, even if we were the unintended victims of their actions.

Next, ask God for help in forgiving them. Forgiveness is a heroic and perhaps even a supernatural act. On our own, it's difficult to truly forgive—we often need to ask for help in doing so. Then, forgive them using the words, "I forgive you." Release them of their debt. It can either be in person or not. It can be communicated to them or not. It all depends on the circumstances. In the process, it might be helpful to communicate the ways in which they hurt you.

Forgiveness is not the same thing as reconciliation, which is the repair to the point where you can continue the relationship in the future. Forgiveness does not mean you are best friends with the person who hurt you, or even that you ever have the same relationship with them again. In fact, it might mean having no relationship with them because it is not healthy. For example, should a woman who was raped and forgives her rapist have a relationship with him? Certainly not. If it's dangerous or unhealthy, there's no obligation for further communication or interaction.

Be aware that your parents might not offer empathy and understanding. It's not unusual for them to become defensive. Why? Perhaps because they feel guilty and ashamed. It's really difficult to admit that you failed or harmed someone, especially someone you love so much. It's very humbling, so their ego might get in the way. It's heartbreaking when parents don't acknowledge and validate your pain. One woman said:[58]

> "When I realized as an adult how much it affected me, I tried to voice my hurt to family members and even my own mother. I was told that I was stuck in the past and that I was too negative all the time. My mother was angry

because she felt she did the best she could and was a victim of abuse by my father.

I never wanted to blame my parents for the ways my pain manifested in my life, I just wanted to feel heard and validated. I wanted an apology, the kind that just simply says, I'm sorry that it caused you trauma and pain. To me, hearing that would have meant in some way that they loved me and were sorry that I spent so many years living in pain. Instead, they were on the defense.

Acknowledging that divorce causes pain isn't putting someone at fault, it's a fact. Being made to feel as though we should just move on is not healthy and can lead to a lot of other issues. I'm so grateful that God has been so close to me as I've been on my healing journey."

If you haven't experienced a response like the one you just read, understand it's a possibility. If you have already experienced this, I'm so sorry. You deserve your parents to understand you and validate your pain.

Be merciful to your parents. Justice means giving someone what they deserve, mercy means giving them what they truly need. Somewhere inside you,

you might want to see your parents suffer. But work on forgiving them and extend mercy toward them. In Latin, the word mercy means "having a heart that is moved at the misery of another."[59] And so, place yourself in their shoes. Try to understand why they are the way they are. It doesn't mean that what happened was okay or didn't matter, but you'll be moved to have compassion for your parents. Compassion will melt the hardness in your heart and allow you to truly love your parents. In fact, it might bring up emotions that you haven't felt in a while, such as pity or sadness about the way your parents are living their lives.

Offering your parents forgiveness will make it easier to nurture your relationship with them and heal any brokenness that affected the relationship as a result of the divorce. There are two ways to grow any relationship: 1) Experiences, and 2) Conversations. Typically, men bond more through experiences, and women bond more through conversations. On the other hand, women typically bond more through conversations. And so, make sure your relationships with your parents have both. Figure out the things that you enjoy and the things that your parent enjoys. Then, do the things that overlap.

Create a mental image of what you want your relationship with each parent to be like. It's very possible you won't be able to achieve the full vision. That's unfortunate, but it's okay. Your mentors can fill that role for you. But do the best you can with what you have in your relationship with your parents. In the end, the goal is to form healthy and peaceful relationships with your parents.

A healthy relationship is impossible without boundaries, so, make sure to set and enforce boundaries with your parents. For more advice on boundaries, listen to this Restored podcast episode: RestoredMinistry.com/36.

QUESTION 28

How do I deal with my parents moving on in life and relationships?

Years ago, I visited a friend's family. The parents are divorced. Though the marriage was annulled, it was still difficult for my friend to see his mom dating again. That weekend, his mom's new boyfriend from out of town visited without my friend knowing he was coming. It made my friend extremely uncomfortable and caused him a lot of anxiety to be blindsided and thrown into what felt like forced bonding.

Sadly, that story is not uncommon. Watching your parents move on is anything but easy, especially when it happens so fast. It might look like watching your parents start dating again or get remarried. Looking for a fresh start, Mom or Dad can even abandon their family for a new family, even if the other spouse stays heroically faithful. Welcoming a parent's new boyfriend or girlfriend into your life is extremely painful and challenging. Building a relationship with a stepparent might be harder than you think it should be, or even feel impossible. You might even realize that Mom or Dad are breaking their wedding vows by the way they are living their life, which is even more heartbreaking. Regardless of the specifics, these scenarios are very difficult to endure.

Your parent's significant other or new spouse brings a whole host of problems and challenges into your life. Especially if that person is around often or moves in with you and your parent. You may feel angry, sad, hurt, trapped, betrayed, as if you don't have control over your life, and completely overwhelmed by all the change and accompanying emotions. You might even feel pressure from your parent to accept this new person into your life right away and to be happy for them. This is neither fair nor realistic. You are entitled to feel everything listed above and more, and to express those feelings. If your parent cannot receive them, divulge your thoughts to a mentor or another adult you can trust. One or both parents can get so consumed by seeking their own happiness and trying to move on from the hurt they experienced, that they overlook the suffering their "new life" causes us. It doesn't mean our parents are bad people or that they don't love us, but we are nevertheless put in a situation that should never happen in the first place. It is not okay, and we are not obligated to pretend that it is.

First, never feel that you need to force yourself to have a relationship with a boyfriend, girlfriend, or new spouse of your parent. You have every right to take that at your own pace. You can be kind and cordial to them, while still holding back from engaging in a relationship with them. If Mom or Dad are forcing or even threatening you to have a relationship with their new spouse, partner, or their children, kindly yet firmly place your boundaries. Tell them what you will and will not allow. If you need space because the person is around all the time or has moved in, pick up a hobby or activity that you will enjoy and will take some time away from home, start working a part-time job if possible, or stay with a friend or family member every so often. It's okay to not be able to handle the proximity of the situation.

Part of the reason it's hard to watch one or both parents move on is that it's not supposed to be this way. Marriage is supposed to be for life. It might sound idealistic, but that's what God originally intended and what the marriage vows promise. When that shatters, it is naturally very disruptive. It's okay to feel that way. If you don't feel comfortable with it, you can admit to them that this isn't how it's supposed to be.

Your parents moving on can also ruin any hope you are holding onto that they would get back together. Subconsciously or consciously, we often hope that our parents might reunite and find a happy ending to their broken marriage. Watching them date and remarry smothers that hope.

If you have concerns about a parent's dating relationship, communicate that to them (see the bonus material for a script on having a difficult conversation at RestoredMinistry.com/bonus). If your parent's significant other or stepparent is mistreating you, don't stay silent. Tell your parents or a mentor. If your concerns are dismissed, place proper boundaries to protect yourself. At the end of the day, your direct influence on your parents is likely very limited. Accept that you have limited control over the situation. It's not your responsibility to be your parents' moral policeman. It's not your responsibility to be the savior of their souls. It's not your responsibility to fix or change them. You can always speak the truth to them in love, but never think that their actions are your fault. They're not. Instead, focus on living your own life. Give yourself what you need—space, time with friends, activities that bring you joy, or even therapy—to cope with this difficult situation. Build virtue, so you can become the best version of yourself and live out God's plan for your life in a heroic way. Heal and grow, so you can feel whole again and experience the joy of living a life fully alive. Your example will speak louder than any words you say. Even when things seem hopeless, remember that God has a plan. This messy situation likely wasn't his original design, but he has a plan that can bring good out of it.

Your Relationship with God

QUESTION 29

Why does God let bad things like my parents' divorce happen?

When disaster strikes, it's natural to question why God would allow such horrible things to happen. Likewise, it's completely normal and understandable to question why God would allow your family to break apart. In the process you may feel like God is far from you or indifferent to your suffering. You may even question his existence. Wherever you are, it's understandable to be there.

Unanswered, those questions are why most people rebel against God. It's typically referred to as "the problem of evil." But this barrier is typically not due to an intellectual argument, but rather an emotional experience. Therefore, intellectual responses can only go so far. While sound arguments can be given to explain why God allows suffering and evil, a perfect sound bite does not exist. Answering the intellectual argument is really less than half the battle.

On an emotional level, I've wrestled with this question for years: God, where were you when I needed you the most? Where were you when my family fell apart? Where were you when the heart of the eleven-year-old me was breaking because of my parents' divorce? If you're all powerful and you could have prevented it, why did you let that happen? Honestly, I felt like he was on the sidelines, watching from a distance. Watching me get beat up, my teeth kicked in.

My answer to this question didn't come at once. It came after lots of prayer, adoration, spiritual direction, and getting to know Jesus personally through Scripture. In time, I learned God wasn't watching from a safe distance. He was right there with me, in the midst of the pain. He was right there with the eleven-year-old Joey whose world had shattered because his parents were getting divorced. He sat in that closet with me, crying and saying: "It breaks my heart too. I don't want it to be this way. But it has to be this way right now." How can that be true? Because of the gift of free will, which people unfortunately use to make decisions that hurt others—whether they mean to or not. Fr. Mike Schmitz taught me that sometimes, God's only response to our pain is his presence. Like a true friend, he endures our pain with us. The best proof that God is in the midst of our suffering is Jesus crucified on the Cross. We can never say that God does not know what it is like to suffer.

On an intellectual level, it's important to understand the difference between God's perfect will and his permissive will. God's perfect will is Plan A. In that plan, Adam and Eve never rebelled. Instead, we lived in perfect relationship with him. But Adam and Eve decided to rebel, which God foresaw since he is all-knowing. He gave them freedom and they chose to use it to go against what he commanded them. You might be thinking: Why would God give us the ability to reject him? Because without the ability to reject him, we couldn't truly love him. Think about it: If someone forces you to love them, is that love? Not at all. It's coercion. And so, if God is all good, then it was necessary for him to give us the freedom to choose between good and evil.

I'll fully admit that it's not easy to understand why God did this. He permits so much pain and suffering. But that's where God's permissive will comes in. Basically, it's not the original design—or what he would have chosen for us—but it is what he allowed us to choose with our free will. And he allows this because he can make good come from it. For instance, Adam and Eve's rebellion against God eventually brought about the world's redemption through Jesus. God literally brought a greater good out of evil. He is so good that he can even use sin in service of his plan.

When faced with intense suffering, these explanations often feel inadequate. It's difficult to fully grasp why God allows natural disasters and deadly diseases when you or someone you love is greatly affected. Even if we understand that all physical evil and moral evil stem from Original Sin, suffering often feels senseless and inexplicable. God's exact reasons for allowing evil are mysterious. But we can be confident that any evil is somehow a result of sin. For God to actively will something that is not good (as opposed to simply permitting it) would go against his nature, which is Truth, Goodness, and Beauty. It is very mysterious, but we can find consolation in the knowledge that this life is not all there is and that God definitively can bring good out of every bad situation—whether we see it or not. Otherwise, despair would be the only option. Heaven exists. This life is a temporary journey. As unsatisfactory as that may sound, trusting God's goodness is the only answer. He is good. He isn't a senseless God. He knows what he's doing. He knows what he's about, so you can trust him as St. John Newman said so beautifully:[60]

> "God has created me to do Him some
>   definite service.
> He has committed some work to me
>   which He has not committed to another . . .
> He has not created me for naught.
>   I shall do good; I shall do His work . . .
> Therefore, I will trust Him,
>   whatever I am, I can never be thrown away.
> If I am in sickness, my sickness may serve Him,
> in perplexity, my perplexity may serve Him.
> If I am in sorrow, my sorrow may serve Him.
> **He does nothing in vain.**
> He knows what He is about.
> He may take away my friends.
> He may throw me among strangers.
> He may make me feel desolate,
>   make my spirits sink, hide my future from me.
> Still, He knows what He is about.

Instead of pushing God away, work through the barriers that hold you back from him and his love. If your hesitance is intellectual, study the arguments that answer your objections. For questions of this importance, you deserve answers. Peter Kreeft's book, *Pocket Handbook of Christian Apologetics*, is a great resource.

If you understand the arguments but your hesitance is emotional, talk with God about it. Spend time meditating on Jesus crucified. Watch the movie, *The Passion of the Christ*. Find a good spiritual director to guide you through those struggles (go to RestoredMinistry.com/coaching).

If you're angry with God, that's understandable. You're allowed to be angry with him. Just make sure you tell him. He can take it. Tell him you feel like he abandoned you. Tell him you don't understand why he didn't intervene. The truth is—he knows what you're feeling and experiencing, but unless we open ourselves up to him, he can't help us. In the end, it will just hurt us and put a barrier up between us and God.

Most importantly, try drawing close to God in your pain. He wants to meet you, right there in the messiness. He likely won't make all your pain and problems vanish, but he will give you the strength to endure them and even thrive in spite of them. For a week, spend time with him for ten minutes a day. Schedule it at the same time and place every day. In time, you'll learn that God's presence in your life is the key to enduring suffering well. And remember that suffering is temporary. It may feel like it has been forever, or you may not see an end in sight, but things will get better—they always do. Even if it's not the way we thought it would be. Hold onto this hope and ask God for the grace to handle whatever suffering you are facing; he is always waiting for us to give him permission.

For more content on this topic, watch two videos from Fr. Mike Schmitz and Chris Stefanick in the bonus material at RestoredMinistry.com/bonus.

QUESTION 30

I feel far from God. How can I get closer to him?

When you're a child, your parents are the most powerful creatures you know. Subconsciously, you believe, "If they're like this, then God must be like this too." In other words, they represent God to you. If your parents harmed you, your image of God is distorted. A distorted image of God causes you to doubt God's love and goodness. The result is that you believe God won't be there for you. He won't take care of you. He won't fill your needs. And so, you don't trust him.

During my parents' separation, I stopped going to church. I hated that God allowed this to happen to my family. Further, I struggled a lot with relating to God the Father since I projected the image and behavior of my dad onto him. My relationship with God was horrible. I fell into despair, feeling that life was hopeless. Even when I did try to reestablish my relationship with God, it was difficult to feel any connection with him. From trial and error, I learned a few things about healing my relationship with God that might be helpful for you.

To undo your distorted image of God, start by articulating what you believe God is like. Often, we never put those beliefs into words. Write it down, including the bad stuff. Then, present it to God. Ask him: God, are you like that? Spend time with him through the Bible and the Sacraments to uncover the real him—not just your distorted idea of him.

Next, identify what's causing you to pull away from him. Is it your anger? Your lack of trust? Your doubt that he's even real? Whatever the reason or reasons, be brutally honest about them. Then, have a conversation with God about those reasons. Tell him everything. Ask him to prove you wrong. Invite him into your heart and life. Ask him to be patient with you as you learn to trust him. He will be.

If you're like me, you've done some stupid things in your past. Sin always separates you from God. It sickens or even destroys God's life within you. It is the cause of all the unhappiness in the world. To start anew, go to confession. If it's been a while, it can be extra intimidating. I remember standing in line for confession after doing some shameful things. I was so terrified and ashamed that I was literally shaking. I was tempted to not go. But the freedom and peace that result from giving God your sins and having him literally wipe them away through his priest are worth it. So often, when you hide your sins, you think you're tricking God. But you're not. St. Augustine said it best, "In failing to confess, I would not be hiding myself from you, but you from myself." In other words, you're just hurting yourself. More than anything, know that God is so good to sinners. Your past doesn't disqualify you from his love. Like the father in the story of the Prodigal Son, regardless of the shameful things you've done, he eagerly awaits your return so he can forgive you and love you (see Luke 15:11–32).

If you've been mistreated by a priest in confession, I am so sorry. It is so wrong. Please know that there are good priests out there who won't shame you but rather will welcome you back with merciful arms. In fact, almost every priest admires the people who confess their sins because they know how much courage it requires. To learn how to go to confession and what to do to prepare, download the app *Confession Guide* by the St. Josemaria Institute or go here to RestoredMinistry.com/confessionguide.

Next, start going to Mass. Go at least on Sunday, but more if you can. Receiving Jesus in the Eucharist is an essential step to healing your relationship with God. Aside from Mass, go to Eucharistic Adoration. To find an adoration chapel near you, search "adoration chapel near me." If you're unable to find one, spend time with Jesus in the tabernacle at a local Catholic church.

Form simple habits that encourage you to pray everyday. For example, determine the time of day that best works for you to pray. Then, designate a place where you will pray every day. If that's at home, you can build a little altar with images or statues of Jesus and the saints. Lastly, make a plan of how you will pray. Keep it simple and allow for some variation. On some days, you might have a lot to say. On others, you might just want to sit with God in silence. One prayer exercise that works for me: I imagine sitting with Jesus on a bench next to a peaceful lake. If prayer is too difficult or distracting, try writing letters to God. Tell him what's happening inside you. Tell him what you want. Tell him what you fear. To learn more about prayer, buy the book *Prayer for Beginners,* by Peter Kreeft or *Time for God*, by Fr. Jacques Philippe. You can also try starting your prayer time by asking God to make the time of prayer fruitful. Then end by thanking God for the time you spent with him.

Learning to trust God is perhaps the most difficult thing to do, but your relationship with him will not improve until you do. In order to trust, we need to discover that he is actually good and trustworthy. A great book on learning how to trust in God is *33 Days to Merciful Love.* In it, Fr. Michael Gaitley shares the spirituality of St. Therese of Lisieux. Instead of focusing on God's justice, she implored and trusted his mercy. She knew that alone, she was weak and sinful. But with God's love and mercy, she could become even a great saint. And she did. In the book, he shares an analogy from St. Therese. She says that growing close to God is like climbing a huge staircase as a little child. Naturally, we cannot do it on our own. It's important to recognize our littleness and our brokenness. But, we should still try to climb the stairs, always trusting that God will come down from the top and carry us up if we simply ask.

To heal your image of God the Father, spend time with good fathers. One priest told me that a great way to heal your relationship with God the Father is by meditating on the life of St. Joseph.

Why? Because he best reflects God's fatherhood on earth. A helpful book for encountering St. Joseph is *Through the Heart of St. Joseph* by Fr. Boniface Hicks. The same is true with good fathers. It could be an uncle, a friend's family, or even a mentor. Aside from St. Joseph, the other saints are incredible mirrors of God's love and goodness. Spend time reading their stories, such as books about Blessed Pier Giorgio Frassati or Blessed Chiara Badano—two saintly and modern young people.

To heal your relationship with God, a spiritual director can also be extremely helpful. A spiritual director is like a coach for your spiritual life. They're not there to control or command you, but rather help you grow in your relationship with God and discern his plan for your life. The difficult thing is finding someone with training in spiritual direction. If you'd like a spiritual director, check out our network of trusted spiritual directors at RestoredMinistry.com/coaching.

You can have a deep relationship with God. Like any good relationship, you have to invest time and effort into it. You can be holy. It's a lie straight from hell to think that it is not possible for you to be a saint. Know that God is pursuing you, even if you don't feel it. He always pursues you. More than anything, he wants your heart. He wants your life. He wants a good relationship with you. He wants you. However, His love is perfect, which means it is never forced. He will not force you into loving him. He wants you to love him voluntarily. He will wait for you.

Decisions and Your Future

QUESTION 31

How can I discern my calling in life when I feel so anxious and uncertain?

When it comes to discerning your vocation or a relationship, you may have been told that you'll know it's the right decision if you feel at peace about it. Any uneasiness is a sign that it's not meant to be. Along those lines, one writer offered this question as a sign that a relationship is not meant to be: "Do you feel anxiety when you think of marrying them?"[61]

But that advice is only half true. A lack of peace could very well mean that this person or vocation isn't for you. But for most people, especially from broken families, it usually requires more digging. In other words, a lack of peace is an important indication that something is happening that is worthy of attention, but it doesn't automatically mean you're pursuing the wrong vocation or dating the wrong person.

In college, I dated a great girl. However, I felt an incredible amount of fear, anxiety, and an overall lack of peace from the beginning of our relationship. It was so overwhelming that I almost interpreted it as a sign that it wasn't meant to be. Thankfully, I dug deeper and realized I was dealing with depression and relationship anxiety. For three months of our relationship, I felt extremely numb and anxious. I could hardly think straight. An argument could be made that I shouldn't have been dating at all—and we did take a break during that time. But had I run at the first sign of a lack of peace, I would've missed out on a beautiful relationship.

The source of my lack of peace was not the vocation of marriage or the woman I dated. It was my fear and anxiety about love, relationships, and intimacy. I was terrified of repeating what I saw in my parents' marriage. I was afraid of opening up about my past and my current struggles. That fear and anxiety interfered with my ability to discern clearly. It blinded me. I felt unable to discern properly. This pattern repeated in most of my relationships, though it got less intense the more I grew.

Another cause for my anxiety was my desire for one hundred percent certainty in my decision to date the girl I was with. I wanted a sign from Heaven. I had to learn the hard way that God doesn't usually make it super obvious what we should do (it would be nice, wouldn't it?). Afraid of making the wrong decision, afraid of failing in the relationship, afraid of repeating my parents' mistakes, I felt so uncertain that I didn't want to decide. It was too dangerous, I thought. Even after I finally made a decision, I second-guessed myself, because I struggled with self-confidence.

The first thing that helped me was to identify that fear and anxiety were at the core of my lack of peace. Therefore, I didn't need to freak out that the relationship wasn't meant to be. Once I knew that, I could start working through my fear and anxiety, so I could see more clearly (see page 50 about handling anxiety). Whenever I felt that anxiety, I learned to be patient with myself instead of immediately doubting my relationship or vocation. So, if you have a similar experience of overwhelming fear and anxiety in a relationship, make sure to question the root of your anxiety. Is it the relationship? Is it this particular vocation? Do you struggle with anxiety? Past wounds? Identify the root of the fear and anxiety that you are experiencing—for people like us, it's often not the external circumstance that is causing it (i.e. the relationship or person you are dating), but rather it is a reaction to past wounds that are being triggered.

Next, don't isolate yourself. Involve older, wiser people who can give you advice and guide you. Share your experience and discernment with people you trust, especially people whose opinion you value. Get their thoughts on whether you and your significant other are a good fit or not. That vulnerability will help you much more than keeping everything secret. That helped me, especially when I couldn't see clearly because of my emotions. So receive the love of others during this time, especially from mentors. This will help you make a better decision and feel confident in that decision. The affirmation and love of a mentor gave me the confidence I needed to pursue my wife.

Beware of your tendency to be a people-pleaser. It won't serve you well when making big decisions. In fact, it will harm you since you might be more interested in making someone happy than in finding what you're called to do with your life.

Naturally, make sure you are praying. It helps to calm your heart, mind, and soul. But more importantly, it helps you connect with God. His opinion and guidance are more important than anyone else's. He knows you better than you know yourself, so get his input too.

Lastly, do your best not to stress about your vocation. Keep your desire to do the right thing and to follow God's will at the center. A pure heart and action will lead you down the right path. When you begin to feel stressed or anxious about your vocation, try praying:[62]

My Lord God,
I have no idea where I am going.
I do not see the road ahead of me.
I cannot know for certain where it will end.
nor do I really know myself,
and the fact that I think I am following
    your will
does not mean that I am actually doing so.
But I believe that the desire to please you
does in fact please you.
And I hope I have that desire in all that I
    am doing.
I hope that I will never do anything apart
    from that desire.

And I know that if I do this you will lead me
    by the right road,
though I may know nothing about it.
Therefore will I trust you always though

I may seem to be lost and in the shadow
    of death.
I will not fear, for you are ever with me,
and you will never leave me to face my
    perils alone.

For more guidance on discerning your vocation, buy Fr. Stephen Wang's book, *How to Discover Your Vocation*. You can also download it for free at RestoredMinistry.com/bonus. Another helpful resource is Fr. Timothy Gallagher's book *Discerning the Will of God*, which is based on the Spiritual Exercises of St. Ignatius of Loyola.

QUESTION 32

I often overthink and feel paralyzed by decisions. How do I fix that?

People like us tend to struggle more with making decisions. Why? There are various factors, but they boil down to one thing: Fear. We're afraid of failing. We're afraid of making the wrong decision. We're afraid of what will happen if we make a certain decision. We're afraid of the unknown that lies ahead beyond this decision. We feel like we can't make a mistake because we believe we're on our own. We have to figure life out ourselves. We can't rely on anyone else to have our backs.

Obviously, fear has an important place in every human life. Without it, we'd likely die by risking too much. But if fear is turned up too loud because of past trauma, it can be truly debilitating. Add a psychological condition such as obsessive-compulsive disorder or clinical anxiety into the mix and it becomes even harder to make good decisions.

As a teen, I remember being paralyzed by decisions. I made decisions slowly, if I made them at all. Sometimes, I'd avoid making a decision altogether. But I realized I couldn't keep living life this way.

Fr. Jacques Philippe gives excellent advice on making *important decisions*. First, he says "faced with an important decision, one of the errors to avoid is that of being excessively hurried or precipitous."[63] When making an important decision, take time to think things through. Don't rush. Analyze the situation. Consider your options. Weigh the advantages and disadvantages of each choice. Ask God for help in making the right decision. Ask advice from wise people you respect. Don't try to do it all yourself. But understand that someone else can't make the decision for you. You must make it yourself.

On the flip side, be careful that you don't treat unimportant decisions the same way you treat important decisions. This is usually where people get stuck. Deciding where to eat or what to wear might feel equivalent to deciding where to go to college, choosing a career, or picking a spouse. That's not good. We need to learn to give each decision the time and attention it deserves based on its importance—no more, no less.

To gain clarity about a decision, talk it out with someone. Write out pros and cons. Remember that most decisions are reversible—you can change course later. The more important and permanent a decision, the more time and attention it deserves. The less important or permanent it is, the less time and attention it deserves.

Often, we need to take a step back from the situation to see it clearly. Navy SEAL commander Jocko Willink told the men under his command to "relax, look around, make a call."[64] Another tactic Jocko recommends is making a small decision down the path that seems best. In many situations, you don't have to fully commit to a decision. You can begin down a path and then change course if necessary. For example, take a girl on a date. You don't need to propose to her yet. Instead of signing up for seminary, just visit the seminary or the religious order. Taking small steps toward a decision helps you have more clarity and make an informed decision.

Feeling overwhelmed is blinding and usually hurts the quality of your decisions. The experience of feeling overwhelmed is typically caused by information overload, the fear of making the wrong decision, the seriousness or complexity of the decision, or stress. An example is buying a vehicle. The options may seem endless and therefore overwhelming. Naturally, it's important to first determine what you will use the vehicle for. In other words, always begin with the purpose or end in mind. From there, you can choose the type of vehicle (car, truck, SUV, etc.) and a brand or two to limit your options.

Highlight the most important factors that matter to you, such as budget, safety ratings, miles per gallon, storage space, or all-wheel drive. Prioritizing those factors from most important to least important to help you make a final call. In essence, you're simplifying a complex decision by breaking it into smaller, more manageable pieces.

After compiling the information based on those factors (perhaps on a spreadsheet or document), give your brain a break to help you see more clearly when you return to the decision. But don't just think through your decision, talk through it with someone. Speaking it out loud will usually help your brain to process the information better, think of things you wouldn't have otherwise, and hear valuable feedback.

Once you've done the hard work of collecting information and truly understanding the options available, a decision should be clear. If it's not, narrow your focus to the most important factors and compare various options. Compare the best option to only one alternative at a time. This saves time by reducing the amount of comparisons necessary. Take time to think it through, but don't wait forever for the perfect decision. Make a call. Albeit inconvenient, you can always sell the vehicle later and buy another if you're unhappy with it, because it is a reversible decision. Always be prepared to learn more after a decision is made and pivot if necessary.

Typically, you won't have one hundred percent certainty in your decisions. Sometimes decisions are clear, but usually you'll have to make a decision with less than one hundred percent certainty. You'll find yourself in situations that are changing, uncertain, and complex. That's when having the ability to make a call in spite of imperfect circumstances is very valuable. In many cases, you'll have to get used to making decisions with seventy percent certainty. In those moments, keep the end goal in mind and move forward with good intentions. Get comfortable with uncertainty. It's not fun, but it's part of life. When deciding, avoid the temptation to find the "perfect choice." Often, it doesn't exist. Instead, choose the best decision. In other words, "Don't make perfect the enemy of the good."

Above all, bring your options, fears, and thoughts to God. Ask what he wants you to do. Sometimes, he'll make it clear. Other times, he won't. In either situation, accept whatever response he gives you and take action.

When making a decision myself, I start by gathering facts about the situation. Then, I try to identify the potential options and weigh those options against each other. Sometimes, the decision is immediately clear. Other times, it is not. I might need to write things out or talk to someone I trust. Once I've given it thought and taken it to God— depending on how important the decision is—I make a call. I can't afford to wait forever for the perfect decision. I have to move ahead.

There are situations in life where there are no good decisions. These are lose-lose scenarios. In those situations, choose the least bad option that minimizes the damage. Of course, never choose a morally evil decision.

Waiting isn't bad in certain situations, but it should be deliberately chosen and not passively fallen upon. Inaction has its own cost too. In a way, it is a decision in itself. Never become like the squirrel that is stuck choosing whether to go right or left. It stands in the middle of the road, unable to decide. At the last moment, it bolts left or right, often to its death.

Perhaps most importantly, know that it's okay to fail. You will make a wrong decision. Nobody has a perfect score at decision making in life. If you make the wrong call, learn from it, adjust course, and make the next best decision. In the words of my mentor, Pat Flynn, "It's better to live a life of 'oh wells' instead of a life of 'what ifs.'" In other words, it's better to give it your best and fail than never try at all.

Be wary of the typical way most people make decisions—we look for the first acceptable option. Sometimes, that's fine depending on the importance and permanence of the decision. But for more serious decisions, such as choosing our vocation or spouse, we shouldn't just choose the first acceptable decision. We should review our options and make a deliberate choice.

If you feel unable to make decisions well, don't despair. With practice, you can learn to make better decisions. You can learn how not to overthink. If I've done it, so can you. Don't let fear dictate your decision making—or lack thereof.

To learn how to become a better decision-maker, start by practicing next time a decision presents itself. First, understand the situation by asking questions and getting all the information available. Next, determine how important the decision is and how permanent it is—is it reversible? Explore your different options—sometimes they aren't all readily apparent. Weigh those options against each other. Take time to think and even talk to someone you trust if it's a big decision. Bring it to God. Then, make a call.

QUESTION 33

Is it selfish or wrong to move on in life and not be as available for my broken family?

In high school, I recognized my parents and five siblings had real needs that I could help fill. I wanted to help them. Thinking of my four young siblings, I knew they needed a father figure. So, I became that for them. Years later, I do believe I helped them grow. Whether it was spending time with them at night, helping them with homework, or whatever else they needed, I knew I could fill that void. I felt so strongly about helping them that I turned down good opportunities and became somewhat isolated from my friends.

When the time came to leave for college, I felt guilty and even selfish. Was I abandoning my siblings? Like most children of divorce, I felt extra sensitive to any form of abandonment. But I knew college was temporary. I'd be home for holiday visits and summers, so I went away to school.

After college, I got a job and moved home. Again, I wanted to be there for my siblings. But I knew that eventually I'd have to move on with my life. At the time, my now-wife Brigid and I were dating long distance. After eight months, we knew we needed to live closer together if we really wanted to determine whether or not we would get married. Again, I felt selfish. But was I?

In time, I realized that no, it was not selfish or wrong. There was nothing wrong with me moving away and pursuing my vocation. In fact, I knew that the best thing I could do for myself and my siblings was to live God's plan for my life. The same is true for you.

The best thing you can do with your life is to become a saint—to live God's plan for your life, especially through your vocation. You can do more good for your parents and siblings by modeling what it means to live a healthy, happy, and holy life than by trying to fix your broken family. It might sound insignificant, but people are watching you. You can be the example for your siblings that shows a good marriage is possible. In fact, that's one of the most healing things for us—witnessing a good marriage and family. So, if God calls you there, build a great marriage.

But this extends to life overall. Seeing a healthy, thriving person inspires others to want the same thing. They just have to figure out how to get there, which you can help with. So focus on your own growth. Follow God's plan. They'll see the joy and peace that you have and want it.

Hearing this, you might think: "My parents and siblings still need help." First, you should always try to redirect your parents and siblings to the proper support. For your parents, that might be a counselor, friend, or family member. For your siblings, that might mean a relative, family friend, or someone at your parish. The goal is to get others to help, especially people who can do so in a healthy way.

There might be a season in your life where you do need to take a more active role in your family. However, it's important that this is only a *season*. It should not be permanent. In the midst of filling that role, you should always set and enforce healthy boundaries with your family members, especially if things get toxic. Helping them should never come at the cost of your own mental, physical, or spiritual well-being.

Even after moving out, you can still love your family in healthy and creative ways. You don't have to be there physically to support them. You can visit. You can stay connected through calls, messages, or letters. You can even do activities together online, like watching a movie together or playing a game.

Staying home and constantly being there for your family might not only be harmful to you, but also to them. You can't do it forever. If they become so used to leaning on you in an unhealthy way, when you eventually have to get some space, it will harm them. It's like pulling the crutches away from someone unable to stand on their broken legs. Relationships like that never end well. Both parties are always worse off in the end. Your parents and siblings need to learn how to stand on their own feet.

In the end, the goal is to develop healthy relationships with your parents and your siblings. Remember that you are not abandoning them by pursuing God's plan for your life. There's no guilt in that. In fact, you're showing your parents and siblings what it looks like to live a healthy, meaningful life. You can still love them from afar.

Naturally, there are some extremely challenging situations people like us face, such as disabled parents. In that case, make sure to ask the help of others in your parents' support system (e.g. family, friends, church friend, counselor, etc.). If you have siblings, the responsibility of a disabled parent should ideally be shared among you.

Do we have an obligation to love our parents and siblings? Yes. But we're not obligated to an unhealthy relationship or to sacrifice living God's plan for us. In following God's plan, we'll best help our parents and siblings by modeling how to live a healthy life and relationships. Had I not taken the risk to move away from my family to pursue my wonderful wife, we would never have built our life together and welcomed our baby girl, Lucy, into the world. Our marriage, and especially our baby girl, have been a blessing to my parents and my siblings.

Ultimately, God's plan is far better than ours. He has an incredible one for your life, figure it out and follow it as best you can. If you do, you'll look up one day and realize what you've built and how far you've come with his help.

If I did, you can too. An adventure full of healing, joy and love are waiting for you. At Restored, we're here to guide you along the way. Learn how on the Resources page below or at RestoredMinistry.com.

Bonuses

To make the book even more valuable to you, we've added free bonus material including:

- Recorded talk and PDF guide, *7 Tips to Build Healthy Relationships and a Divorce-Proof (Future) Marriage*
- Step-by-step guide for how to have a difficult conversation with your parents.
- Additional tips for how to practice good self-care to help you feel and be your best.
- Extensive playbook of healthy coping ideas that are easy and fun.
- Questions for small groups discussions.
- List of every recommended resource from the book in one easy location.

Get the bonus material in three easy steps:

1. Scan the QR code below or go to RestoredMinistry.com/bonus.
2. Enter your name and email.
3. Get access to the bonus material!

Resources

Restored exists to serve teenagers and young adults from broken families. We offer the practical guidance and support they need to heal and grow, so they can feel whole again. We do so through our content, coaching, and community.

Content

Podcast

Practical lessons from stories and expert interviews that help you heal. To listen, go to RestoredMinistry.com/podcast

Blog

Stories and advice that help you become healthy and whole. To read, go to RestoredMinistry.com/blog

Speaking

Live or virtual presentations for schools, conferences, and churches that offer practical guidance to young people from broken homes. To book a talk, go to RestoredMinistry.com/speaking

Books

Books and booklets to offer guidance on navigating the pain and problems from your parents' divorce, separation, or broken marriage. To purchase, go to RestoredMinistry.com/books

Coaching

Free national referral network of counselors and spiritual directors that we vet, trust, and recommend. To find a coach, go to RestoredMinistry.com/coaching

Community

Free and private online community with people like you who actually get you, support you, and help you become a stronger person. Join our community at RestoredMinistry.com/community

Social & Email

- Follow us on Instagram @restoredhelp
- Join our email list at RestoredMinistry.com/email

Feedback

If you believe this book would help more young people, would you take 3–5 minutes to leave an Amazon review? Great reviews make the book more visible on Amazon, which helps us reach more young people.

1. Sign in to Amazon.com or the Amazon Shopping app
2. Navigate to Your Orders
3. Find the book
4. Select "Write a product review"
5. Rate, write your review, and select Submit

If you have any issues, email Support@RestoredMinistry.com.

Any feedback on how we can make this book better? Fill out the 2–3 minute survey at RestoredMinistry.com/booksurvey

Help Young People from Broken Families

"As the family goes, so goes the nation and so goes the whole world in which we live."
—Saint John Paul the Great

To help us reach thousands of young people from broken families, would you consider making a donation?

Our content helps young people from broken families to heal and build virtue, so they can form healthy marriages and strong families. You can make a donation in three simple steps:

1. Scan the QR code below or go to RestoredMinistry.com/donate
2. Choose your donation amount and frequency
3. Enter your name and payment info

If a monthly donation is given, an account will be created for you. You can stop or adjust your donation at any time. If you have any issues, email Support@RestoredMinistry.com.

Restored is a 501(c)(3) charitable organization. All contributions are tax-deductible to the fullest extent allowed by law. Thank you so much!

Notes

1 Pennebaker, James W., and John Frank Evans. *Expressive Writing: Words That Heal*, 30. Enumclaw: Idyll Arbor, 2014.

2 Fagan, Patrick., and Rector, Robert. "The Effects of Divorce on America." The Heritage Foundation. Heritage.org. Accessed June 29, 2021. https://www.heritage.org/marriage-and-family/report/the-effects-divorce-america

3 Amato, Paul. "Children of Divorce in the 1990s: An Update of the Amato and Keith (1991) Meta-Analysis." *Journal of Family Psychology*, 2001, 360. https://doi.org/10.1037/0893-3200.15.3.355.

4 Blakeslee, Sandra, and Julia M. Lewis. *The Unexpected Legacy of Divorce: the 25 Year Landmark Study*, 329–36. Hachette Books, 2001.

5 McBroom, Patricia. 09.05.00 - Historic UC Berkeley study finds profound impact on adult lives of children 25 years after their parents' divorce, 2021. https://www.berkeley.edu/news/media/releases/2000/09/05_divorce.html.

6 Frankl, Viktor E. Essay. In *Man's Search for Meaning: An Introduction to Logotherapy*, 38. Beacon Press, 2006.

7 Charen, Mona. *Sex Matters: How Modern Feminism Lost Touch with Science, Love, and Common Sense*. Crown Forum, 2018.

8 Mal 2:16 *New American Standard Bible*. Chicago, IL: Moody Press, 1977.

9 "*Catechism of the Catholic Church: With Modifications from The Editio Typica*, 2383. New York, NY: Doubleday, 1997.

10 Ibid.

11 Miller, Leila. "When Does the Church Tolerate Divorce?" Catholic Answers. Catholic.com, February 20, 2019. https://www.catholic.com/magazine/online-edition/when-does-the-church-tolerate-divorce.

12 Ibid.
13 Ibid.
14 "*Catechism of the Catholic Church: With Modifications from The Editio Typica*, 2384. New York, NY: Doubleday, 1997.
15 Miller, Leila. "When Does the Church Tolerate Divorce?" Catholic Answers. Catholic.com, February 20, 2019. https://www.catholic.com/magazine/online-edition/when-does-the-church-tolerate-divorce.
16 Pope John Paul II. "Familiaris Consortio (November 22, 1981): John Paul II." Familiaris Consortio (November 22, 1981) | John Paul II. Vatican.va, n.d. https://www.vatican.va/content/john-paul-ii/en/apost_exhortations/documents/hf_jp-ii_exh_19811122_familiaris-consortio.html.
17 Ibid.
18 United Families International. "Myth Buster Monday: Parents Who Have Conflict in Their Marriage Should Divorce for the Sake of Their Children." Unitedfamilies.org. United Families International, January 31, 2011. https://www.unitedfamilies.org/parents/child-development/myth-buster-monday-parents-who-have-conflict-in-their-marriage-should-divorce-for-the-sake-of-their-children/#_ftn2.
19 The Code of Canon Law (1983), c. 1137. Accessed August 14, 2023. https://www.vatican.va/archive/cod-iuris-canonici/eng/documents/cic_lib4-cann998-1165_en.html.
20 Marriage and Family Life Ministries. "Annulment." USCCB. Accessed June 24, 2021. https://www.usccb.org/topics/marriage-and-family-life-ministries/annulment#tab--what-does-the-tribunal-process-involve.
21 Ibid.
22 Civitci, Nazmiye, Asım Civitci, and Ceren Fiyakali. "Loneliness and Life Satisfaction in Adolescents with Divorced and NonDivorced Parents." *Educational Sciences: Theory and Practice*, 2009, 518. https://doi.org/513-525.
23 Halvorson, Heidi G. "The Cure for Loneliness." Psychology

Today. Sussex Publishers. Accessed June 29, 2021. https://www.psychologytoday.com/us/blog/the-science-success/201010/the-cure-loneliness.
24 Ibid.
25 Ibid.
26 Stillman, Jessica. "Happiness Makes Your Brain Work Better." Inc.com. Inc., February 27, 2012. https://www.inc.com/jessica-stillman/happiness-makes-your-brain-work-better.html.
27 Pontarelli, Joey. "#047: How Healing Improved My Life, Marriage, and Friendships: Sandra Howlett - Blog." Restored. Restored, June 22, 2021. https://restoredministry.com/blog/047.
28 "Dictionary." Google Search. Google. Accessed June 24, 2021. https://www.google.com/search?q=confidence&oq=confidence&aqs=chrome.0.0i433l3j46i433j0i131i-433j0i433l2j69i61.1068j0j7&sourceid=chrome&ie=UTF-8.
29 Blakeslee, Sandra, and Julia M. Lewis. Essay. In *The Unexpected Legacy of Divorce: the 25 Year Landmark Study*, 329–36. Boston: Hachette Books, 2000.
30 Young, Adam. "2 Why Your Family of Origin Impacts Your Life More Than Anything Else." Spotify. The Place We Find Ourselves, April 17, 2018. https://open.spotify.com/episode/6jriLq9km69DER1RggiNOM?si=67a025aef84f4dc4&nd=1.
31 Ibid.
32 Ibid.
33 Ibid.
34 Frankl, Viktor E. Essay. In *Man's Search for Meaning: An Introduction to Logotherapy*. Beacon Press, 2006.
35 Chapman, Gary D. *Anger: Taming a Powerful Emotion*, 53. Chicago, IL: Moody Publishers, 2015.
36 Astrup, Aske, Carsten B. Pedersen, Pearl L.H. Mok, Matthew J. Carr, and Roger T. Webb. "Self-Harm Risk between Adolescence and Midlife in People Who Experienced Separation from One or Both Parents during

Childhood." *Journal of Affective Disorders* 208 (2017): 582–89. https://doi.org/10.1016/j.jad.2016.10.023.

37 "Self-Harm." Crisis Text Line, June 23, 2020. https://www.crisistextline.org/topics/self-harm/#what-is-self-harm-1.

38 Ibid.

39 "Talk To Someone Now." Suicide Prevention Lifeline. Accessed June 28, 2021. https://suicidepreventionlifeline.org/talk-to-someone-now/.

40 David, Susan. *Emotional Agility.* Penguin USA, 2018.

41 Achor, Shawn. *The Happiness Advantage: How a Positive Brain Fuels Success in Work and Life.* New York: Currency, 2010.

42 Wojtyla, Karol. Essay. In *Love and Responsibility,* 112. Ignatius Press, 1993.

43 Parrott, Les, and Leslie L. Parrott. *Saving Your Marriage before It Starts: Seven Questions to Ask before—and after—You Marry,* 15. Grand Rapids, MI: Zondervan, 2006.

44 "XIX World Youth Day, 2004: John Paul II." XIX World Youth Day, 2004 | John Paul II. Vatican.va. Accessed June 28, 2021. https://www.vatican.va/content/john-paul-ii/en/messages/youth/documents/hf_jp-ii_mes_20040301_xix-world-youth-day.html.

45 Parrott, Les, and Leslie L. Parrott. *Saving Your Marriage before It Starts: Seven Questions to Ask before—and after—You Marry,* 15. Grand Rapids, MI: Zondervan, 2006.

46 Parrott, Les, and Leslie L. Parrott. *Saving Your Marriage before It Starts: Seven Questions to Ask before—and after—You Marry,* 121–124. Grand Rapids, MI: Zondervan, 2006.

47 Institute, Arbinger. *Anatomy of Peace: Resolving the Heart of Conflict.* 3rd ed. Berrett-Koehler, 2022.

48 Lewis, C.S. *The Four Loves,* 121. San Francisco, CA: HarperOne, 2017.

49 "'Downton Abbey' Episode #6.5." IMDb. Accessed August 16, 2021. https://www.imdb.com/title/tt4574910/characters/

nm1890784.
50 Wagner, Stephen, and David Lee. "Abortion: From Debate to Dialogue—An Interactive Guide." JFAweb.org. Justice for All, 2015. http://doc.jfaweb.org/Training/ADD/ADD_IG_Three_Essential_Skills.pdf.
51 Parrott, Les, and Leslie L. Parrott. *Saving Your Marriage before It Starts: Seven Questions to Ask before—and after—You Marry*, 117–134. Grand Rapids, MI: Zondervan, 2006.
52 Parrott, Les, and Leslie L. Parrott. *Saving Your Marriage before It Starts: Seven Questions to Ask before—and after—You Marry*, 32. Grand Rapids, MI: Zondervan, 2006.
53 Young, Adam. "The Place We Find Ourselves: How Stories of Harm Lead to Agreements That Bind Us on Apple Podcasts." Apple Podcasts, August 12, 2019. https://podcasts.apple.com/us/podcast/how-stories-of-harm-lead-to-agreements-that-bind-us/id1373926216?i=1000446697182.
54 Ibid.
55 David, Susan. *Emotional Agility*. Penguin USA, 2018.
56 "Dave Ramsey Twitter Page." Twitter . Twitter, September 21, 2016. https://twitter.com/daveramsey/status/778566341229969408?lang=en.
57 "Daniel Tardy Instagram." Instagram. Accessed June 28, 2021. https://www.instagram.com/p/CPLg5wbhnbu/.
58 "Restored Instagram ." Instagram. Accessed June 28, 2021. https://www.instagram.com/p/CNDV5hKjTHq/.
59 FOCUS National. "Sr. Miriam James Heidland, SOLT & Fr. John Burns: 'Seeking Healing Through Forgiveness' | SEEK2019." YouTube. YouTube, January 5, 2019. https://www.youtube.com/watch?v=l8rVfw013TQ.
60 Newman, John Henry. "The Mission of My Life." John Henry Newman—Prayers. John Henry Newman Catholic College. Accessed August 12, 2021. https://www.johnhenrynewmancatholiccollege.org.uk/john-henry-

newman-prayers/.

61 "The Devil Wants You To Settle in Your Relationship." Chastity.com. The Chastity Project, May 27, 2015. https://chastity.com/2014/02/the-devil-wants-you-to-settle-in-your-relationship/.

62 Mostardi, Joe. A Prayer of Unknowing by Thomas Merton. Augustinian Spirituality, May 5, 2021. https://augustinianspirituality.org/2020/11/27/a-prayer-of-unknowing-by-thomas-merton/.

63 Philippe, Jacques. In *Searching for and Maintaining Peace: a Small Treatise on Peace of Heart*, 70. New York: Alba House, 2002.

64 Willink, Jocko, and Leif Babin. *Extreme Ownership: How U.S. Navy SEALs Lead and Win*. Sydney, N.S.W.: Macmillan, 2018.

Made in United States
Orlando, FL
23 November 2024

54342063R00134